BURE
MOTOR-CYCLE DRESS

Worn and recommended by the Misses Nancy and Betty Debenham, Authors of "Motor=Cycling for Women"

Burberry dress protects the motor-cyclist from neck to boots, and spells finality in

SECURITY, COMFORT AND EFFICIENCY

The outrig illustrated consists of a Tielocken Burberry Motor-cycle Coat, which provides double protection over all the vital areas of the body, and Breeches.

Made in Burberry Gabardine, this outfit

KEEPS OUT RAIN, WIND AND COLD

yet is airylight and naturally ventilating ; cool for summer riding, yet, owing to the extreme density of the materials, snug and warm on the coldest day.

Catalogue, and patterns of Burberry Gabardine and other Motor-cycling materials, sent on request.

BURBERRYS Ltd. HAYMARKET LONDON S.W.1

ARIEL

THE MODERN MOTOR-CYCLE
NEW PRICES

5·5 H.P. SIDE VALVE STANDARD MODEL	A	£43 :	10
5·5 H.P. SIDE VALVE DE LUXE MODEL	B	£46 :	0
5·0 H.P. O.H.V. STANDARD MODEL	C	£48 :	10
5·5 H.P. O.H.V. DE LUXE MODEL	D	£50 :	0
5·0 H.P. O.H.V. SUPER SPORTS MODEL	E	£52 :	10

PARTICULARLY SUITABLE FOR LADY RIDERS

RELIABILITY 5,000 MILES WITHOUT ONE ENGINE STOP

AND

EXTREMELY LOW RIDING POSITION

ARIEL WORKS, Ltd.   SELLY OAK BIRMINGHAM

WHY YOU SHOULD BUY AN ARIEL

£43 10s.  £43 10s.

5·5 H.P. SIDE VALVE STANDARD MODEL A

PROVED
AND
IMPROVED
WITH
THIRTY-TWO NEW FEATURES

Catalogue  *from*

ARIEL WORKS, LTD. SELLY OAK BIRMINGHAM

(5487)

A Splendid New Work of Reference for Owner-Drivers and Riders

CARS & MOTOR-CYCLES

EDITED BY
LORD MONTAGU of BEAULIEU·C.S.I.,K.C.I.E.
& MARCUS·W·BOURDON

In the present work is given clear and reliable information regarding the driving and management of cars and motor-cycles. The information is presented in such a way that it can be understood by anyone without any previous knowledge of the subject, either on the technical or driving sides. No attempt has been made to deal with engines or vehicles of any particular make, as it would be quite impossible in a work of this kind to keep up to date with this rapidly growing industry. As far as possible the work has been confined to the main principles which undergo little or no change over a period of years. It is this feature which will make the complete work so valuable as a work of reference.

NOW BEING ISSUED IN FORTNIGHTLY PARTS

Price 1/3 each
from a Newsagent

Details post free on request

Sir Isaac Pitman & Sons, Ltd., Parker St., Kingsway, W.C.2

The VILLIERS Two Stroke is the most reliable engine made

—consequently a motor-cycle with this engine is the most suitable for Ladies. The Villiers engine generates its own Electric Light, so providing a *fully equipped* machine at a very small extra cost. The following motor-cycles are fitted with Villiers two-stroke engines.

BAKER	GRINDLAY-PEERLESS
CEDOS	JAMES
COTTON	McEVOY
COVENTRY-EAGLE	N.U.T.
DIAMOND	ROYAL RUBY
DOT	S.O.S.
EXCELSIOR	SUN
FRANCIS-BARNETT	ZENITH

Send a Post Card for full details

THE VILLIERS ENGINEERING CO. LTD.
MARSTON WORKS = = = WOLVERHAMPTON

1928 MODELS AND PRICES

Model K.1. 7·99 h.p. de Luxe Passenger Combination with Dynamo Lighting Set, Electric Horn, Mechanical Lubrication **£95 0 0**

Model K.2. 7·99 h.p. Standard Passenger Combination with Mechanical Lubrication .. . **£80 0 0**

Model K.3. 3·49 h.p. de Luxe Touring machine with Mechanical Lubrication **£47 0 0**

Model K.4. 3·49 h.p. de Luxe Sporting machine with Mechanical Lubrication **£47 0 0**

Model K.5. 3·49 h.p. Standard Sporting machine **£43 10 0**

Model K.6. 3·49 h.p. O.H.V. Sporting model with Mechanical Lubrication. Twist Grip Control to Carburettor . . **£50 0 0**

Model K.7. 3·49 h.p.O.H. Camshaft machine. Dry Sump Lubrication. Twist Grip Control to Carburettor. **£62 0 0**

Model K.8. 4·98 h.p. O.H.V. machine. Mechanical Lubrication. Twist Grip Control to Carburettor ... **£59 10 0**

Model K.9. 4·98 h.p. de Luxe Touring machine. Mechanical Lubrication. Twist Grip Control to Carburettor ... **£55 0 0**

Model K.10. 4·98 h.p. O.H. Camshaft machine. Dry Sump Lubrication. Twist Grip Control to Carburettor. **£73 0 0**

Model K.12. 2·48 h.p. Lightweight machine. **£39 17 6**

Any A.J.S. Machine can be obtained on Hire Purchase Terms.

May we send you Catalogue and fuller information?
A. J. STEVENS & CO. (1914) LTD., WOLVERHAMPTON.
LONDON DISTRIBUTORS : H. TAYLOR & CO., L

EMINENTLY SUITABLE FOR ALL PURPOSES

A MOTOR-CYCLE is by far the most efficient form of light transport, either for business or pleasure; its uses being unlimited, whilst on the points of Capability and Economy it scores over every other kind of mechanically propelled vehicles.

The choice of a machine must, however, be made wisely; features to be considered being Ease of Management and Control, Accessibility, and, above all, Reliability.

The A.J.S. has always been famous for its road performance and unequalled service—therefore, in selecting this make you are safe in the knowledge that you have chosen a machine to give you entire satisfaction.

LONDON SHOWROOMS: 122-124 Charing Cross Road, W.C.2
TD., 49-53 Sussex Place, South Kensington, S.W.7.

Decarbonizing —a nuisance

Avoid it this easy way

NEW motor-cyclists can—from the start—avoid frequent decarbonizing by using only Golden or Triple Shell— the *proved* Anti-Carbon motor-cycle oils.

Old motor-cyclists can avoid frequent decarbonizing from now on. Carbon feeds on carbon—increases until speed and power diminish. Decarbonize—then start afresh with Anti-Carbon Oil!—and use no other.

The high Anti-Carbon value of Shell Motor-Cycle Oil was conclusively proved by the Shell 2,000-mile A.C.U. observed trials—twelve different standard models travelled at cruising, hill-climbing and race track speeds.

The Official A.C.U. Report said: "In every case the (carbon) deposit was not so much as to require a removal for efficient running, was black in colour, oily, and of such a consistency that it could be removed without difficulty with a scraper of hard wood."

the anti-carbon oil

MOTOR-CYCLING
FOR WOMEN

THE
MOTOR-CYCLIST'S
LIBRARY

This new series is intended for all interested in motor-cycling. Each book in the Library deals with a particular type of motor-cycle from the point of view of the owner-driver. The necessary preliminaries, the essentials of good driving, running, upkeep and repair, and also useful legal and general information are all treated with special reference to the particular make of motor-cycle with which each book deals.

"Gives just the information people want.' —*The Sketch.*

THE BOOK OF THE B.S.A. By "Waysider." Second Edition.

THE RALEIGH HANDBOOK. By "Mentor."

THE BOOK OF THE DOUGLAS. By E. W. Knott.

THE BOOK OF THE TRIUMPH. By E. T. Brown.

THE BOOK OF THE ROYAL ENFIELD. By "R. E. Ryder."

THE BOOK OF THE A.J.S. By W. C. Haycraft

THE BOOK OF THE RUDGE. By L. H. Cade

THE BOOK OF THE P. & M. By W. C. Haycraft

"Ripe and expert experience placed at the disposal of the novice for a trifling sum."
—*Venture.*

Each, Price 2s. net. Of Booksellers

London : Sir Isaac Pitman & Sons, Ltd., Parker St., Kingsway W.C.2

Frontispiece THE AUTHORS *For Photos*

MOTOR-CYCLING FOR WOMEN

A BOOK FOR THE LADY DRIVER, SIDE-CAR PASSENGER, AND PILLION RIDER

BY
BETTY AND NANCY DEBENHAM

LONDON
SIR ISAAC PITMAN & SONS, LTD.
PARKER STREET, KINGSWAY, W.C.2
BATH, MELBOURNE, TORONTO, NEW YORK
1928

Published by
classicmotorcyclemanuals.com 2015
Reprinted 2017

Stephen Brown © July 2015
5 Quarry Lane
South Shields NE34 7NJ
0191 435 4122

ISBN 978-1-908890-12-2

Reproduced by Shore Books and Design
Blackborough End, Norfolk PE32 1SF

Printed by Biddles Books
King's Lynn, Norfolk PE32 1SF

Introduction

The year this book was written was a period of great optimism; 62 nations renounced the use of war to resolve disputes and the sun shone, a fortnight in July that year recorded temperatures of 90 degrees and no rain. Significantly 'Motorcycling for Women' was published in 1928, when women achieved an equal voting age with men at 21. The book reflects a golden period when there were more motorcycles on the road than cars and anyone could ride a motorcycle at 14 without passing a test or wearing a helmet.

You will see from the photographs in this book that the authors Nancy and Betty Debenham were attractive, adventurous and happy young ladies who thoroughly enjoyed their motorcycling. The sisters became poster girls for BSA motorcycles in 1927. However, they were also hardy, tough, brave, knowledgeable and resilient motorcyclists in their own right and not just selected for their looks. Indeed, Nancy won a Gold Medal at Brooklands Racetrack in 1926. They were often accompanied on their journeys by their little dog Poncho who would sometimes stowaway in the sidecars and cars of strangers.

They were part of a small but very enthusiastic band of female motorcyclists who took part in all kinds of motorcycle events; including gymkhanas, trials and journeys to foreign parts.

By modern standards the sisters escapades in riding a sidecar outfit with a few minutes training, finding a certain lack of brakes and clutch and tying the sidecar on with rope would give a present day health and safety officer a heart attack. However, I'm sure none of these events were particularly unusual in the twenties.

Perhaps some of the more enlightened manufacturers saw the equalisation of the voting age as a chance open up a new market at a time when motorcycle sales had dipped due to the introduction of cheap cars such as the Austin 7. This book seems to be part of a concerted campaign by British Motorcycle Manufacturers to promote motorcycling for women. However, in his introduction Major Watling (Director of the British Motorcycle Manufacturers Union) manages to reveal something of the prevailing attitudes to women motorcyclists at the time: 'Whilst none would wish the fair daughters of Eve to emulate the example of rude Adam at Brooklands or the Isle of Man' and 'motorcycling is well suited to the daintiest face and most elegant figure…it is not now only the enthralling occupation of the dirty handed schoolboy'.

Although some manufacturers produced ladies models and promoted women riders on official factory brochures this did not result in large scale sales. Indeed women only occupied 4% of the market in the UK.

Overall 'Motorcycling for Women' is a Cheery, Practical guide to Motorcycling in the 1920's written by two sisters who just loved motorcycling.

My thanks go to Julie from the Sunbeam Club for her help and to Nigel for his patience in preparing this book. A special thank you goes to my friend Brian Wedge for his proof reading skill's. Thanks also to all those who have bought my books and given such positive feedback.

Thanks also to Anne Peacock of Pearson Publishing for her help in trying to establish publishing rights on this book.

PREFACE

WE have derived so much pleasure from our own motor-cycling experiences that we feel it is our simple duty to write of them, and enable other road lovers to share with us our joys.

We hope that it will be useful to would-be riders, and also to girls who already have tasted the thrill of motor-cycling, either as drivers or passengers.

Any helpful suggestions that may be found within its pages are the result of actual experience, painful and otherwise, and these hints may assist others to avoid some of the pitfalls into which, from time to time, we have fallen.

B. and N. D.

Beauty "On the wheel"

O^N the question of fuel the points which most appeal to the lady motor-cyclist are "snappy acceleration," "pick-up," "mileage," "clean running," and "easy starting."

That is why she always chooses Pratts Spirit.

*Uniform everywhere
—reliable always.*

D.A. 47

CONTENTS

CHAP.		PAGE
	PREFACE	v
	INTRODUCTION	ix
	(By Major H. R. Watling, Director of the British Cycle and Motor-cycle Manufacturers' Union)	
I.	"THE MAGIC CARPET"	1
II.	SIDECAR TOPICS	5
III.	OUR FIRST SIDECAR TOUR	9
IV.	HOLIDAY TOURS	12
V.	CAMPING WEEK-ENDS	18
VI.	WEEK-END RAMBLES	22
VII.	BY ROAD TO RIVER	25
VIII.	FROCKS AND FRILLS	29
IX.	MOTOR-CYCLING AND HEALTH	33
X.	THE ROAD GIRL'S COMPLEXION	36
XI.	THE PILLION PASSENGER	38
XII.	"TWO UP" ON TOUR	43
XIII.	THE "SOLO" RIDER	47
XIV.	LEARNING TO RIDE	51
XV.	ON CHOOSING A MOUNT	55
XVI.	THE NEW MACHINE	59
XVII.	REPAIRS, REPLACEMENTS, AND ACCESSORIES	62
XVIII.	ROAD SENSE	65
XIX.	THE LAW AND THE LADY RIDER	68
XX.	CLUBS AND THE SOCIAL SIDE	71
XXI.	THE ART OF TRIALS RIDING	75
XXII.	CONCLUSION	81

BY WAY OF INTRODUCTION

BY

MAJOR H. R. WATLING

(*Director of the British Cycle and Motor-cycle Manufacturers' Union*)

THE appearance of this book is significant of the growing interest in motor-cycling amongst women, who with acute feminine intuition, appreciate the part that a motor-cycle can now play in their lives. To-day a woman shares in sport and business, in social affairs, and public government as does a man. It is, therefore, only natural that she should now utilize weapons first forged for him alone, and which by strenuous test have exhibited their use in all life's purposes. Of such weapons transport is the chief, and in transport the motor-cycle is indeed pre-eminent.

The motor-cycle has a worthy past and an honourable and a useful present. It preceded the motor-car, and by the motor-car it has never been superseded. For the individual it remains a unique mode of transport. Its development proceeds, and its usefulness increases day by day. As it caters for all classes and all demands of manhood, so, too, it has become the handmaid of womanhood. Whilst none would wish the fair daughters of Eve to emulate the example of rude Adam in his thrilling headlong career at Brooklands or in the Isle of Man, yet—in the hundred and one humdrum uses to which the motor-cycle can be put in daily life—for recreation, health, pleasure, social affairs, and business—the motor-cycle has become an almost necessary equipment of women of all ages.

"Freedom" is the essence of modern womanhood, and the motor-cycle is one of the gifts of the gods whereby such is attained. No longer is she dependent upon caprice of husband or brother— no longer is valid the "thou shalt not" which erstwhile debarred her from indulging in his activities—no longer does distance prevent her from full enjoyment of her multifarious interests— the motor-cycle is her servant—to carry her as she wills. It is her protector—the motor-cycle is her iron chaperon—no longer need she pine for lack of opportunity to indulge in outside interests—the motor-cycle provides for her needs.

It is the function of the authors to guide womanhood in the art of driving a motor-cycle, but let me here say that it is simple in operation, easy in control and balance; it possesses neither the whimsies of horse-flesh nor the discomforts of train or coach.

Although motor-cycling already finds favour with the modern girl, as yet its value has not been generally appreciated throughout all grades of feminine society. Its sphere of usefulness to women in all occupations can greatly be extended, and the purposes in which a motor-cycle can serve them the authors of this valuable work admirably and clearly convey to inquiring minds.

The schoolmistress, nurse, journalist, and secretary can be conveyed with safety and celerity; the time and fatigue of the housewife can be saved; the pleasure of the "sports" girl can be lengthened by the time saved in conveyance to and from the golf course and the tennis club. All this, too, apart from the hundred ways in which time and money can be saved by the use of a motor-cycle in the ordinary affairs of everyday life.

Motor-cycles are manufactured in all types to suit every purse and purpose. There are those light and economical machines which should appeal particularly to any of the fair sex who has just reached years of discretion and judgment. That age (as a mere man knows) comes very soon. Indeed, I fancy that in fixing the age limit for issue of motor-cycle licences at 14 years Parliament must have foreseen the extension of the motor-cycling movement in the manner now reviewed by the authors!

Already the motor-cycle has made dreams of travel and adventure a reality. Witness Lady Warren's description of her journey with her son, so well described in *Through Algeria and Tunisia*, and Mrs. Clare Sheridan's adventures in Bolshevik Russia, admirably depicted in *The Cruise of the Satanella*. Both these journeys were successfully undertaken by women on British motor-cycles and sidecars.

And every trust can be placed in the British motor-cycle. Sturdy in construction, yet light; capable of negotiating all gradients, yet easily controlled and manoeuvred; economical and safe in use; a suitable mechanical Sir Galahad; a modern Knight who awaits his Ladye's commands.

No better exponents of the practical gospel of motor-cycling could have chosen the task of writing this book than its charming authors, who have a first-hand knowledge of its every aspect, and can show how motor-cycling is well fitted for the daintiest face and most elegant figure—that it is not now only the enthralling occupation of the dirty-handed schoolboy.

In the confident expectation, therefore, that you will find pleasure and profit in reading the wise advice of its authors, I willingly commend this book to your acceptance.

MOTOR-CYCLING FOR WOMEN

CHAPTER I

"THE MAGIC CARPET"

LESS than a score of years ago the motor-cycling Eve was a strange creature, who wore her oldest clothes and a strained expression of uncertainty. Lady riders were rare, and the majority of women, if they did venture on a trip, did so as a sidecar passenger, and what a sidecar, to be sure! It was not likely to be the beautifully upholstered affair of to-day, with its elaborate springing and shock absorbers, but a box-like contraption which quivered and shook with every vibration. Wind-screens were practically unknown, and part of the "fun" of a sidecar journey was to arrive home very filthy or quite often not to arrive home at all, for in these early days motor-cycle engines were unknown quantities, and likely to leave the owner stranded miles away from anywhere.

Taking all these discomforts into consideration it can hardly be surprising that most women preferred a stay-at-home existence, while their men-folk indulged in these uncertain journeys alone.

Nowadays things are different. The ease with which even a novice can manage the modern motor-cycle, its simplicity and reliability, make it an ideal means of transport. It is the magic carpet of the town dweller.

Eve has forsaken her old prejudices, and accompanies Adam on his travels. She does not turn a hair when he tells her to be ready in half an hour to go away for the week-end, but calmly packs as much as possible into one small suitcase and is quite likely to be ready before him.

She knows that she will not have to freeze all night by the roadside while the engine is taken into small pieces and put together again. She knows that she will be warm and comfortable, and she has perfect faith in the driver and machine. In fact, she knows it will be a joyride.

The town dweller has no need to go far away to be in the heart of the country. There are usually delightful spots within 25 miles radius of any big town. The Londoner is particularly lucky in this respect. He has the sea within fifty miles, and two hours' riding will bring him into the New Forest or the Surrey hills.

When planning a tour a large-sized road map is essential. Maps may seem very complicated, but they are really quite easy to follow. The best kind is planned on the lines of the Ordnance Survey map, and shows the Ministry of Transport first and second class roads and road numbers all printed in colours and very

Fig. 1. "In the New Forest"

simple to read. "Dear me, how dull!" some might say, "To plan a tour by the aid of a map!" but, dear rider, this is the only way to ensure a tour's success. A haphazard trip usually ends in failure. The mere fact of asking the way every few miles is sufficient to spoil it, and it is unsatisfactory to never know where to stop for the night. Even if it is a success a glance at a map *after* a tour of this kind is sufficient to see what a much better route could have been chosen.

A list of the towns on the route should be made before starting off. The Dunlop and Michelin guide books are useful when choosing a route. They contain sectional maps marked with the mileage between different towns, and they also include lists of recommended hotels with descriptions of their accommodation and advantages.

The new rider will naturally start with main road tours, but having gained experience, Eve and her escort can forsake the beaten track and explore the by-lanes. Every good road is crowded with traffic during the week-ends, and it is a relief to turn into the shade of some little-used country lane. Even if the going is bad it does not matter, for to understand the art of joyriding one must never be in a hurry, and the world will not come to an end even if the days average mileage is low. The beauty of the country will more than make up for the bumpy state of the road.

There are little-known roads along the Kentish cliffs on the way from London to Canterbury which are well worth trying. They are crossed at intervals by the arterial roads which are cut like scars across the face of the country, but the joy-rider avoids these, leaving them to people who are merely anxious to " get there." The bleak perfection of the arterial roads often cheats the motor-cyclist of his real enjoyment of the countryside. He sees a signpost pointing to his destination and follows it blindly, only to find that an arterial road has performed a surgical operation on the prettiest parts of his route. One passes through no picturesque villages, and the only landmarks are dangerous cross-roads and garish new filling stations. These roads are fine for transport, and relieve the older roads of the heavier traffic, but please, if you are out on a " joy ride," don't acquire the " get there " habit. Cultivate, instead, the gentle art of appreciation, and explore the by-ways.

The A.A. and R.A.C. road services have made it possible for Eve to travel alone, or with a woman companion, without any fear of being stranded without help in the event of a breakdown, for every few miles one sees gleaming amongst the trees the welcome yellow sign which reads " *A.A. Telephone* 1 *mile*," while along every main road there are to be found A.A. and R.A.C. mechanics who tour the highways, and act in the capacity of roadside Guardian Angels, and are called upon to do anything from rendering first aid in the case of an accident to giving help in capturing a roadside thief. They help with any repair job, and as well as being first-class mechanics, they play the parts of walking encyclopaedias, answering questions on all sorts of subjects, advising tourists as to the best routes and hotels, and generally making themselves indispensable to the roadfarer.

Every motor-cyclist should join the A.A. or R.A.C. The advantages of belonging to these bodies are well worth the small yearly subscription, including as they do a " get-you-home " scheme, free legal advice, help over insurance matters, and numerous other advantages. They will even take on themselves the task of mapping out your holiday route, giving you maps and tour lists, and the names of the best hotels to stay for the night.

The A.A. and R.A.C. hotels can generally be relied on to be comfortable and reasonable in price, while recently the " R.A.C. Inn " has come into being, where they serve meals at 2s. per head, and make a speciality of catering for motor-cyclists. These inns are usually not so large as the listed hotels, and rather more homely and rustic, just right for the motor-cyclist, who does not want to change for dinner, but prefers to eat a comfortable " high tea."

CHAPTER II

SIDECAR TOPICS

GREAT care should be exercised in the choice of a sidecar. First it must be decided how many passengers it usually will be expected to carry ; whether it is to be a family " bus," or a sporting little affair for two, with somebody occasionally on the carrier.

The wisest course, once having settled on the type, is to buy the outfit complete. It is a great mistake to buy a machine and then tack the sidecar of one's fancy on to it. For one thing it costs a lot more buying them piecemeal, and then the balance may be wrong. Too much strain, as likely as not, will be imposed on the couplings, and the whole outfit be less satisfactory than if it is purchased complete.

Makers invariably know the exact requirements of their models and what to recommend in the way of a chassis, so, if you or a member of the family already have a machine, and are desirous of becoming sociable by fitting a sidecar, that is quite a different matter. It is certainly wise to get into touch with the makers and have one of their sidecars fitted, or, if they don't happen to make them, they will recommend the right type for their make of machine.

Personally, from varied experience, we prefer the roomy family body to the sporting torpedo shape, that seems to call for the assistance of a shoe-horn to get us in or out. They look beautiful, of course, and for a run of a few miles they are comfortable enough, but not for a long journey. It is absolute agony if one is travelling all day not to be able to change one's position except in the slightest degree, and the weather and the dust have it all their own way.

No, the roomy, solid, comfortable type for us, even if it is not so smart and dapper as the stream-line model.

Then there is no room for luggage in the ultra-smart torpedo ; the long tapering back prevents any possibility of a luggage grid, and the best you can do is to stuff things loose in the toe and heel, with, of course, the addition of a suitcase on the carrier. But the sidecar with the locker and the luggage grid is capable of carrying the whole family wardrobe if necessary.

The B.S.A. Co. make a two-passenger model, which is delightfully comfortable. It weighs 235 lb., and is priced about £27. It has separate wind-screens for both occupants.

This is travelling in comfort with a vengeance, but if something smaller is required, there is a single-seater with a locker which can be converted into a seat for a child. This weighs only 160 lb., and is fitted with a really effectual wind-screen, spring seats, and all home comforts. The present price of this is £19.

For those who prefer a sporting body there is the Rudge-Whitworth with a tiny wind-screen, price £20, or the semi-sports, which is really quite comfortable, and boasts a very practical wind-screen. The price of this is £18.

The choice of a sidecar is all such a matter of taste and experience, but for long distance touring our advice is, choose something that is really weather-proof and by a maker of repute.

It is so discouraging to sit in a pool of water day after day if you happen to strike a bad patch of weather, whereas if you are warm and dry and well protected, you can radiate a cheeriness that will communicate itself to your driver, even though he is bearing the brunt of the storm. Not that there is any need for the rider to get wet and miserable in these days of weather resisting devices. Large and efficient wind-screens can be fitted to the combination, which in conjunction with wide legshields and side-flaps, ought to keep the rain out. The only thing that is lacking is a roof, but on some of the latest designs in windscreens there is a slanting section which goes over the rider's head and can be adjusted at will.

For those who already possess a sidecar which needs weatherproofing, such as the ultra sporting body with no cover, there is a tiny collapsible hood which can be folded up and carried in a pocket of the sidecar when not in use. This is thoroughly rain-resisting, and buttons down to the sides to the wind-screen, and the passenger snuggles down in comfort and warmth. Various firms make pneumatic cushions which are invaluable for long journeys. It is so useful to be able to inflate them according to requirements, and a small sized cushion fitting into the small of the back takes away that tired ache one is so prone to after a few hours on the road.

The girl driver of a combination is well catered for to-day. Time was when she had to exercise all her muscles to control a heavy outfit, struggling to handle a fierce clutch, and generally wearing herself out. She then arrived home feeling her trip had done her more harm than good. But nowadays, high-powered machines are so silky and tractable, that the prospective buyer, however frail in physique, need have no hesitation on the score of power or weight. This advice is only in connection with combinations. In another chapter we explain that the small girl or the novice should content herself with a lightweight.

Olympia at show time is the place to see the sidecar of one's dreams. And the best plan for people who can manage it, is to go to the Motor-cycle Show and make a choice.

Fig. 2. "A Sidecar with Locker and Folding Luggage-grid"

Fig. 3. Off for a Fortnight's Holiday

Cinderella coaches in every conceivable shade are to be found there, some fitted with little dashboards, with vanity case and mirror complete. One we saw had a complete picnic equipment fitted into the well at the back. Spirit stove and kettle had their little niches, and needless to say, the whole arrangement could be taken out to make room for more serious luggage for a protracted tour.

There is a sidecar on the market which can be used as a bed, and two of them are being used in a trip round the world.

Truth to tell, the lay-out of this outfit is far from beautiful, but certainly has its uses. It is built on the long side, and has a collapsible mattress made on the air cushion principle, which forms the upholstery during the daytime. The sidecar is rather flat and low in shape, and the bed is built on top of it. It has a tent which is easily erected over the sleeper. The idea is, that the dangers of sleeping on the ground in foreign countries are numerous, and this is a way of overcomng them. So, for our readers contemplating a motor-cycling holiday abroad, this is a scheme well worth considering, but in good old England, in fine weather, a sound tent and ground sheet are very much simpler.

CHAPTER III

OUR FIRST SIDECAR TOUR

ONE of our first experiences with a sidecar outfit involved a journey of nearly a thousand miles. Save for a driving lesson of five minutes duration in one of the London parks (our instructor being in a terrific hurry) we had never handled a combination.

However, we set off blithely enough, taking the dog as a special treat. " Poncho " is a sturdy little dog of doubtful pedigree, and we named him after our black rubber raincoats because he is always getting wet. His hobbies are swimming and motoring, he will flop into any handy patch of water, swim madly round and round, and then come and shake himself all over our clean stockings.

His passion for motoring makes him lose all sense of loyalty, and he will even go for long drives with perfect strangers. One summer some friends took him for a tour, and when he was brought back he pretended not to know us, but sat bolt upright in the car and carefully examined something on the opposite side of the road. Yet usually he is most unhappy when away from us, and pines to see us again, but such is the effect of a motor ride that nothing else matters. When we go away without him he spends all his time in the garage, sitting in strangers' cars and hoping they'll take him out with them.

We started off without realizing that a sidecar outfit uses more than a solo, and consequently we ran out of petrol before we had covered 50 miles. Luckily, we were near the top of a hill, our combined efforts pushed the outfit over the brow, and we coasted gently down to the village at the foot.

It was a very small village, but we found a cottage which apparently did a roaring trade in lemonade and sweets, with petrol as a side issue. A kindly old lady handed us a green can, with the remark that her husband was out, so we were our own garage man, and proceeded to fill the tank.

Then with smiles and thanks we attempted to go on our way. Nothing would induce our mount to start. We kicked and kicked, took out the plugs, found them perfectly clean, and put them back ; wondered vaguely about the magneto and carburettor, and fell back on kicking again. Never having had any previous trouble we were rather at a loss as to what we should do next.

A kindly car owner appeared on the scene and gave us a tow, saying the machine would be sure to start then, but nothing happened. At last, when we were almost in despair, the owner of the green can came home, and made inquiries as to our trouble.

We told him, and a look of horror came over his face as he hurriedly asked his wife where she got the petrol from. When she said " Behind the door in the shed " he explained that he had taken in a load of paraffin that morning, had filled a petrol tin and put it apart from the others, so that it should not be used.

Our friend with the car and some of the villagers emptied the tank, even turning the outfit upside down so that not a drop of such objectionable liquid should remain. This done, we filled up with real petrol, and the good natured engine started first kick, after her usual fashion.

This incident serves to show that it is a great mistake to buy petrol at wayside cottages and sheds. We have always made a point of seeing that we have enough in the tank to pick and choose where we shall get more, since that warning.

We got along very well after that, considering the machine of ancient vintage we had borrowed possessed all sorts of drawbacks for the handling of a novice. For one thing the sidecar was far too light, and had been hurriedly tacked on for our benefit. The clutch would not disengage, and the brakes needed relining ; yet we were mad enough to set off for Wales with all these disabilities. If was our lack of experience that made us so confident. Nowadays we should be aghast if anyone suggested our undertaking a long journey without some adjustments to such a decrepit and elderly concern.

We had several remarkable escapes from turning it over. Once it actually did capsize, pinning the driver underneath, while the passenger and dog flew gaily overhead into a hedge. No damage was done except that Poncho's feelings were so hurt that he raced on to the next village, where we found him awaiting our arrival.

This little disaster sobered us up considerably, and we proceeded at the dignified gait of 15 miles an hour for most of that morning.

Our destination was Aberystwyth, and we had made up our minds to reach there on the second day, but the foregoing incident slowed us up so much that we found ourselves climbing Plynlimmon in the fast gathering dusk. But for a few sheep sleeping peacefully here and there on the road, this was a scene of uninterrupted loneliness. We took one hasty glance at the sheer drop to the valley beneath on one of the sharp turns, and then, all the way up that lengthy mountain, we preferred to keep our eyes rigidly fixed on the road ahead. All went well until we reached the top, but on the way down an unpleasant grating sound made itself heard. The passenger shone her torch over the side where the noise seemed to come from, and found to her horror that the

OUR FIRST SIDECAR TOUR

sidecar seemed on the point of leaving the machine, the very insecure couplings having come adrift.

Our inadequate brakes being quite incapable of bringing the machine to a standstill, and, in any case, there being no possibility of assistance in that desolate waste, we descended as slowly as we could, the passenger hanging on to the carrier for dear life, to keep body and soul together.

After what seemed like years we reached the foot in safety, and we carried on until we came to some cottages where we obtained a stout rope, and with some help lashed the afflicted parts together. In due time we arrived in Aberystwyth, and succeeded in rousing our hotel, the occupants of which had long since gone to bed. During our stay we had a special bolt made which kept the outfit together until our safe arrival back in London.

We accomplished the journey home to the accompaniment of a few small excitements—for instance, having no clutch, we had to run with the machine to start it, one holding the bars and the other vigorously pushing the sidecar. When it eventually sprinted off we had to get aboard as best we could, the passenger occasionally landing on her head in the sidecar, and straightening her ruffled self as we went along. This performance caused a little amusement here and there, and annoyed us intensely. It caused us to pass all the places where we longed to stop, and all the nice cafés where we were sure they supplied glorious meals, and we would eventually pull up at some lonely uninteresting cottage, and be fed on the everlasting ham and eggs. All because we did not want an admiring crowd to watch us start off.

The absence of the clutch was our bitterest reproach to the kind owner of the outfit on our return, while he, on his part, was so thankful to see us back, safe in wind and limb, that he forgave us all the scars and other injuries we had inflicted on his precious steed.

CHAPTER IV

HOLIDAY TOURS

ONE of the amusements of a motor-cycling holiday is the interesting task of mapping out a tour; although many people are inclined to be bewildered by maps and like to have things arranged for them.

It is for these lazy souls that we have prepared a few routes, with London as a jumping-off point.

The Lake District wants a lot of beating for sheer beauty, and the lover of gorgeous scenery would do well to spend at least one holiday in these perfect surroundings.

The two main roads out of London which lead to the Lakes, although excellent for the man in a hurry, are exceedingly dull. And since our holidaymaker wants to enjoy every moment of her, trip, we advise leaving London by way of Watford, Tring, Bicester and Banbury; on through the picturesque old town of Warwick and pretty Kenilworth. By this road we miss the bustle of Coventry, and we arrive by excellent roads at the Stonebridge Hotel, a very good place to stop and have a meal. On resuming, we keep straight across the main road, so avoiding Birmingham, and going through Nuneaton and Ashby-de-la-Zouch, we reach Derby.

Of course, there are quicker routes, but if time is immaterial it is well worth while going the prettiest way.

After Derby one is obliged to encounter a few towns which do not add to the beauty of the scene; still they might be worse, and it is possible to skirt some of them. The country outside these dull little industrial towns is really lovely.

Leaving Derby we take the road to Chesterton, and thence through Sheffield and Barnsley. Leeds is quite a pleasant town, and after that the glorious Yorkshire Moors. Taking the road to Ilkley and Otley, we pass through Skipton, Long Preston, and come to Kirkby Lonsdale. Next we arrive at the quaint old town of Kendal, and now we are on the threshold of the Lakes.

Windermere or Ambleside would be delightful places to stay, or if it is preferred to get farther into the wilds, Cockermouth is lovely. The beautiful little town where Wordsworth was born is well worth exploring, with its picturesque old ruined castle and Gothic buildings.

We once spent a very entertaining three days with Cockermouth as our headquarters. We found an extremely comfortable little hotel in the High Street, where they fed us royally at an inclusive charge of 10s. 6d. each a day. Large bowls of cream with our porridge, too, because they kept a farm as well as an inn. Windermere and Ambleside, famous for their beauty, are very expensive to stay in. Coniston is a dear little place on the shore of the lake, and far from being pretentious like some of the better known beauty spots, it offers very reasonable charges. Then there is a wee village comprising a handful of cottages and about one shop, called Holmground, where we found a marvellous farmhouse. They charged us £2 10s. each for the week, including all meals. And

FIG. 4. RESTING BY THE WAYSIDE

such meals! Great jugs of cream instead of milk, home-made jams, and all sorts of good things.

It overlooks Scafell and the purple heights of Helvellyn. Here there are many mountain paths where it would be impossible to drive a motor-cycle, but they are well worth climbing on foot. The glorious views from some of these vast heights have to be seen to be believed.

Outside Cockermouth the road to Bassenthwaite can be taken, where there is a marvellous view of majestic Skiddaw, and the return journey can include lovely Derwentwater, and by digressing for a few short miles one can see Borrodale and the Falls of Lodore.

For sheer hard-going the road over Wrynose Pass and Hard Knott to Wastwater takes some beating. In some places it is little better than a river-bed boulder strewn, and with many a sharp turn and steep ascent, but if plenty of time is allowed it can be accomplished with a fair degree of comfort.

All the way there are beauteous scenes to feast the eye, and

Wastwater, surely the most awe-inspiring spot in its isolation and grandeur, is well worth all the difficulties of getting there.

There is also a beautiful little place to stay in named Hawkshead. This is an absolute picture village with centuries-old cottages in white stone with black beams, and the gardens are a dream of delight. The humblest cottages are blest with Adams doors and fire-places, and the whole place is ablaze with flowers. It has been untouched by time and, even without the intention of staying there, is well worth a visit.

Having dilated on the glories of Lakeland, we will turn our attention to a tour which will take us farther afield, namely, to the wilds of Scotland. Starting from Kendal—for there is no reason in the world why our tourists should not at least have a glimpse of the Lakes on the way—we proceed by way of Shap to Penrith.

Most of our readers who have done any touring will know Shap. It was considered quite a formidable hill at one time, when motor-cycles were not what they are to-day. It is a long lonely mountain road, very bleak and desolate, but with an excellent surface, and coasting down the other side for several miles, it does not seem to take any time before one arrives at Penrith.

Carlisle is the next town of any note, and soon we see a sign telling us we are about to cross the Border.

There is quite a thrill in first setting foot or wheel in Scotland, and there is some very pretty country to be traversed on the way to Edinburgh, but it is when one travels north of the famous city that one begins to see the majesty and grandeur of the country. But we have not reached Edinburgh yet, and the road we like best is the one through Longtown, Langholm, Hawick, Selkirk, Innerleithen, and Peebles. If this is our reader's first visit to the Scottish Capital, it is essential to stay a day or two in order to explore its marvellous castles and points of interest. But if all these have already been seen, one gets along to Queensferry, and takes the boat across the Firth. Once across, there is a choice of routes. One can either go by Dunfermline and Alloa and the beautiful Bridge of Allan, on through Callander to Lochearnhead (this is a good place to put up for the night, by the way), through Killin, Kenmore, Aberfeldy, and join the road from Perth at Ballinluig, or one can go direct to Perth.

The road round by Callander is very much longer, so, of course, it depends how much time one has to spare, but if it is possible, it is much the pleasanter way.

The main road to Perth embraces some dreary little mining villages and some very ill kept roads. By the other road we come out between twenty and thirty miles above Perth on the way to the Grampians. Now we are really getting to the scenery. After

HOLIDAY TOURS

Blair Athol the loneliness and rugged grandeur have it all their own way. For a stretch of 20 miles or so there is not a sign of human life, nothing to be seen but an odd mountain sheep or two. Of course, in the summer it is perfectly beautiful, but in the winter it is a very different story. We once reached Braemar as a snow storm was blowing up, and were advised to hurry up the mountain pass before the Devil's Elbow became impassable. As this was

FIG. 5. THE FAMILY GIRL

the shortest way to Perth by more than a hundred miles we made up our minds to try to get through.

We simply couldn't manage it, though blinded and battered, we struggled as far as the Devil's Elbow, which is a hairpin bend in a hollow which fills with snowdrifts, only to sink hub deep and stick. Our united efforts lifted our little mounts out of this morass, and we were just about to try again, when a car which had toiled up the pass, strongly advised us to turn back. "You'll never get through" said the driver, "it gets worse farther on, I know this road, and I'm not attempting it," and he proceeded to turn his car. We went back to Braemar, and found a very comfortable cottage, and stayed there two days before the storm abated, and even then we had to go the long way round.

However, this is a summer tour and these excitements are not likely to happen. At Dalwhinnie, a tiny desolate village, there is a fork road to the left, which leads to Drumcask, and then one gets on a most romantically picturesque road for miles and miles to the Spean Bridge Hotel, and then along the shores of wonderful lochs. Here yellow irises grow in profusion, and the views are simply beyond description. It would be a good idea to make headquarters somewhere about here, and start out each day in different directions, otherwise it is impossible to really see the superb scenes on every hand. Fort William is quite a nice little town in which to stay, and there are queer rickety ferrys to carry you and your outfit across the lochs at various points.

One could easily spend a month in this district and never get tired of exploring the lochs, or get satiated with their beauty.

It is possible that our tourists would like to go farther north. In that case, instead of leaving the road at Drumcask, it will be necessary to carry on through Newtonmore, Kingussie, Carrbridge, and on to Inverness. We made this charming old town our headquarters on one visit to Scotland, having found how very comfortable they made us at the Imperial Hotel. From there we visited Strahpeffer (this is a beautiful place to stay, also), and made a day tour to Loch Maree, which is one of the show-places of Scotland.

The roads are very rough and flinty when one gets as far west as Auchnasheen and Jeantown, and tyre trouble is rather prevalent, so it is necessary to take a good puncture outfit. There are so many miles of loneliness with never a glimpse of a friendly garage to offer a helping hand, that one might be stranded for hours without the necessary tools. A puncture is a small matter, especially when two people get to work on it, so adventurous Eve must not be cast down by this little homily on bad roads, but just be safeguarded.

It is an undisputed saying that good scenery means bad roads, and from our experience we have certainly found it true.

Nevertheless, we would infinitely prefer traversing pot-holes and cobbles amongst the lochs, to bowling monotonously along the Great North Road.

If one has a fancy for following some almost uncharted country, it is possible to go on from Jeantown to Applecross. It is necessary to go with caution, as a mountain path has to be descended. It is very rough and steep, with acute hairpin bends, and attention should be paid to one's brakes before attempting it. It can be imagined how bad the going is when one hears that this road is rarely used, the quaint little fishing village of Applecross, which nestles at its foot, being visited by steamer once a fortnight.

This is the inhabitants' sole link with the world.

It is well worth visiting, if the descent can be negotiated; it is such an extraordinary contrast to everyday life.

The bathing here is excellent, and a few days leading the simple life with the fisher folk on what is almost a primitive island would be a Crusoe-like experience to garner in the storehouse of memories.

Climbing the steep mountain out of Applecross with its hairpin bends will provide another thrill, and if there is time to spare, one should turn sharp left at Auchnasheen, almost doubling on one's tracks, to gain the road to Loch Maree.

From Auchnasheen to Loch Maree is less than 20 miles, and it would be a pity to miss the breath-taking loveliness of this tremendous lake. Several hours could be spent traversing the fairylike shores, and then a comfortable jog back would bring our tourists into Strahpeffer for dinner. This is a charming little town in which to spend the night, or if it is necessary to push on, the road through Carrbridge into Inverness is excellent.

Anyone getting so far into the West of Scotland as we have been in this chapter would naturally want to spend all the available time there, but on the way back, a pause at the well-known Pass of Killiecrankie must be allowed for. This lovely place simply calls for admiration as does the quaint and beautiful little town of Pitlochry.

After the sheer beauty of the highlands it seems a little hard to have to descend to the mundane level of the Great North Road, but if the close of the holiday is drawing near it is by far the quickest way to London.

Two days should suffice for the journey. We always make a point of reaching Leeming Bar, a village near Boroughbridge, for our night's rest where we know a little inn named " The Sun," where they make us extremely comfortable for a very small charge, and where we have a tender recollection of liqueurs at sixpence a head.

Leeming Bar is just about half way, so that it should be easy to arrive in London in time for dinner on the second day.

So ends as magnificent a holiday as could possibly be wished for, and enough memories and incidents to talk over to last the whole winter, or at least, till the next opportunity for a jaunt comes round.

CHAPTER V

CAMPING WEEK-ENDS

CAMPING-out has a charm all its own. It sounds very unpoetical, but there is nothing quite so delicious as the scent of bacon frying outside one's tent on a fine summer morning.

The open-air girl might rave about the scent of honeysuckle or sweet briar, but if she was candid she would admit that this was her favourite camping-out scent.

A camping week-end can nowadays be made very comfortable, especially if one is the lucky owner of a sidecar outfit. Collapsible tents can be had that fold up into a ridiculously small space and these, with ground sheets and air cushions, make very comfortable travelling homes.

A cyclist's tent can be hired at any of the big stores for about 7s. 6d. per week, and the price for buying outright varies from 18s. 6d. to as much as four guineas. A more expensive tent is a better investment than a cheap one, as it is made of stronger and more lasting material, but even the ones that cost under a sovereign last a long time with care. Never roll up a tent when it is damp, if it can possibly be avoided, as this will rot the canvas, shortening its life considerably. A spirit stove is useful during these damp summers, especially when camping by the river. It may not be as picturesque as a wood fire, and if the weather is hot and dry, then by all means try your hand at camping gipsy-fashion, but remember to take your spirit stove as well.

It is not necessary to take all the way from home everything in the way of provisions. Hard-boiled eggs and unperishable things can be brought with you, but it is better to buy in a village near the camping place the bread, butter, salads, and other things that spoil easily.

It is just as well, before pitching the tent, to see that there is a handy water supply; it is a small point, but one often forgotten by newcomers to camp life. Also be sure you are not camping on private ground unless you have first asked permission. Remember that politeness pays, and that half a crown and a smile given to the right person at the right time might save all sorts of unpleasantnesses later on. Farmers are very touchy when trippers are rude to them, and rightly so ! After all, it is their land, and they are doing you a favour in letting you use it as an open-air boarding house.

Of course, it is not always possible to know when one is

CAMPING WEEK-ENDS

FIG. 6. CAMPING DE LUXE WITH THE RUDGE CARAVAN

20   MOTOR-CYCLING FOR WOMEN

trespassing. We were once on a holiday of this sort and we pitched our tent amongst the sandhills near the sea. It was getting dusk, for we had been pottering for some time along the coast admiring the sunset, and it was not until we were preparing breakfast next morning, and a golf ball landed almost in the frying pan that we realized we had pitched our tent in the middle of a bunker right on the golf course!

When camping-out always take a first-aid outfit, including iodine, boracic lint, and bandages. Even an insect bite, or a small

FIG. 7. PONCHO ASKS "IS BREAKFAST READY?"

cut may become dangerous if it is neglected, and should receive immediate attention. A bottle of Condy's fluid is another useful addition to the medicine chest.

Then there is the question of crockery. It may seem extravagant to buy special sets of picnic ware, but they would soon justify their original cost in the amount of breakage they save. Then there are the paper plates and cups that can be thrown away after use, all very useful and labour-saving.

All these are Eve's affairs, and while Adam attends to the mechanical needs of his steed Eve can look after the comfort side of the picture, and providing they each look after their own job it is a splendid way of spending a week-end.

There are wonderful camping grounds near London. People

CAMPING WEEK-ENDS

who live on the South side naturally make for Surrey. There are spots in the New Forest, and even as near London as Newlands Corner, that are so peaceful that one might be hundreds of miles from Town. In Surrey in the Spring there are buttercup fields of gold, and fairy rings on which the grass is so green and fine that it hardly looks real. Later on in the year, when Nature rolls up her golden carpet and puts it away until the next year, she throws on to the deep green grass purple patches of heather and handfuls of scarlet poppies. Surrey is a county of extravagant beauty and violent contrasts.

Those living on the Eastern side of the town need hardly be told of the unspoilt beauties of Epping Forest, where there are more shades of green in the trees than there are anywhere else. People call Essex flat and uninteresting, but we prefer to call it beautiful and restful, with its cool, deep forest and its leafy lanes.

On every side of London there are routes within easy reach, later on we will deal with longer tours, but these are quite far enough for a week-end camping holiday.

Prospective campers ought to join the Camping Club. Their address is Tudor House, Princeton Street, Bedford Street, London, W., and they offer all sorts of facilities for the modest sum of 10s. per year. This includes a magazine devoted exclusively to camping matters.

There is the Rudge caravan, which is small and light enough to be towed by a six horse-power sidecar outfit. It is a most compact little travelling home, and has two beds, and all the necessary furniture stowed away in its tiny interior. It is a good investment for the tourist who wants to use her outfit all the year round, for one can be quite cosy in it during the colder weather. It is nicely built and balanced, and easy to move from place to place.

CHAPTER VI

WEEK-END RAMBLES

ONE of our favourite week-end trips is to the Bognor and Selsey coast.

Taking the route through Guildford, the most beautiful road is through Godalming to Haslemere. Here, only about forty miles from London, one might be in the heart of Devon. The road rises and dips, giving unexpected twists and turns. On the heights there are wonderful views of four counties, while in the valleys there are little cameo scenes of cottages and gay gardens.

Midhurst is the next place on the route, and this also is a joy, although perhaps rather spoilt and self conscious, as if too many people had admired it. Here there are picturesque hotels that are rather spoilt by being obviously show places. At least fifty famous people seem to have made the place their favourite haunt, and their bedrooms and special corners are duly labelled and put on show.

We prefer the simplicity of the " Dog and Duck," which is a *real* country inn near Singleton, a little village a few miles farther on.

Here they have a lovely garden, all ablaze with old-fashioned flowers and sweet with the scent of herbs, and here on a fine summer's afternoon one can have tea, with lettuces freshly gathered, and home-made jam.

Proceeding to Chichester, and then on to Bognor, the road winds through green, park-like scenery right away to the coast.

It is only 63 miles from London, and it is one of the prettiest roads in England.

When we go this way we never stay in Bognor itself, because we know of an excellent hotel called the Richmond Arms at Waterbeach, near Goodwood. This is a wistaria-covered inn situated almost at the foot of the Silent Avenue, a green-canopied road leading up to the racecourse, so called because no birds ever sing in its trees.

Except at race meeting times this hotel is very quiet and reasonable in price. They charge something under 10s. for an excellent supper, bed, and breakfast.

There is an alternative route back to Town which is well worth trying, for it takes you through such interesting places. Arundel and Fittleworth are two of them, and they are both worthy of a few hours delay on the homeward journey.

Sometimes we go farther afield. One fine week-end we decided

FIG. 8. WE PAUSE NEAR STRATFORD-ON-AVON

to visit Shakespeare's Country and the river Avon, so we looked up a route on our map, packed a small attaché case, and started off in our sidecar outfit, taking with us our faithful hound Poncho.

We went through Maidenhead and Henley, and on through the charmingly named Nuncham Courtenay to Oxford. Aristocratic double-barrelled names seen to be fashionable on this route, for we passed through Chipping Norton, Moreton-in-the-Marsh, and Boughton-on-the-Hill. We stopped at the top of the winding switchback known as Fish Hill and admired the view. It was apple-blossom time, and the landscape looked for all the world like a delicate Japanese water-colour. It was wonderful! We stayed there quite a long time before coasting slowly down the hill into Broadway, which is known as the prettiest village in England. Certainly nothing could have been lovelier than the masses of fruit blossom against the green, and the thatched cottages with their gay gardens, but to our hungry eyes the sight of a real country tea which was spread before us in one of the cottages was almost as good.

We were so intrigued with our cottage that we stayed the night. It had none of the pretty show-place atmosphere, but was just naturally comfortable and homely. So many of these cottages are traps for the unwary. If you stop there for tea they are quite likely to serve up musty eggs and plum and apple jam. We were up very early the next morning, and were given an excellent breakfast, over which we discussed our plans for the day. We finally decided to go fishing in the Avon at Evesham, and then potter home in the afternoon. We had never had any experience as anglers, but we were always willing to learn.

At Evesham we found an obliging boatman who agreed to supply us with tackle and rods, but then we came across a difficulty. " I doubt if you'll catch anything with that there dog," he said, pointing at Poncho, who was swimming in the river, registering his approval by barking at the top of his voice, " 'is noise 'ud scare the fish for miles," and after a little further discussion we abandoned our plans and went for a walk along the towpath. On the way back we suddenly discovered that Poncho was missing, we hurried back to the sidecar in alarm and there he was, trotting unconcernedly away from it. The next thing we noticed was a peculiar smell, and after a short search we found that the smell belonged to a peculiarly large and horrible bone that Poncho had " buried " for future use in the nose of the sidecar.

Needless to say, he was *not* allowed to travel it!

We lunched at Stratford-on-Avon, and after a short sightseeing trip we turned our outfit homewards, going back by way of Warwick, Banbury, and Aylesbury, and arriving home, rather tired but full of fresh air, at about eight o'clock that night.

CHAPTER VII

BY ROAD TO THE RIVER

AFTER the dust of the road it is sometimes very nice to drift down a quiet backwater in a canoe, or lounge at ease in a punt, and a river week-end makes a welcome change from the country or the coast.

The motor-cyclist, being independent of trains, has no need to follow the crowd to Maidenhead or Henley. There are little riverside villages which have no railway station and only one small boathouse; they are too small to have an important place on the largest map, and one comes across them only by accident.

There are places like this on the banks of the river Wey, a winding capricious little river which has never grown up. It is one of Father Thames' many children, and it drifts amiably through Guildford and Godalming, finally losing itself somewhere in the wilds of Hampshire. The village of Send, near Ripley, is a good starting-off place if one wishes to explore the river Wey.

At Send it is possible to hire a boat for the whole day for a few shillings; there is no railway station, and it only has one inn, but this is an " R.A.C. Inn " and very good. We found it quite by accident, one hot Sunday last summer, when we turned off the crowded Guildford road in search of peace and quiet. Having lunched royally at the inn, we found our way to the boathouse and hired a dinghy.

We followed the course of the river for three miles. It wound in and out like a silver ribbon in a flower-decked mantle of green. Sometimes we rowed through cool green tunnels formed by the willow-trees where they met overhead, and at one point the narrow stream widened into a still blue pool, so clear that it would have formed a mirror for Narcissus himself, and we could fancy that behind the trees lurked shy nymphs and dryads, who timidly resented our intrusion.

Apart from the people of our fancy, we were absolutely alone, and even the cattle and horses in the fields seemed to be under a fairy spell, for they were so still and quiet.

At the second lock, which is about three miles along the river from Send, we used the lock-keeper's cottage as a dressing room and had a swim, for in the summer we never go off for the whole day on our motor-cycles without taking our bathing costumes, and having spent ten minutes in the clear water, we dressed ourselves and went for a brisk walk along the country lanes in search of tea, and it was then that we discovered why the people at the inn had tried to persuade us to take a tea basket, for not a soul amongst the cottagers would provide us with any ! In desperation we held a consultation with the local milkman, who was on his round, but he sadly shook his head " They don't encourage trippers round these parts," he said. " But you might try that cottage, tell Mrs. Smith the milkman sent you." We knocked at the door of a rambler-covered cottage, but Mrs. Smith was not at home. Another passer-by told us to try the hotel at the cross-roads, but this was worse than ever, and nothing could have been more unwelcome than the shut doors of the " Green Goat." Having had a council of war with the garage man opposite the hotel, who advised us to walk another mile along the main road, we made our way back to the river, and, finally, begged some people who lived on the banks to make us a pot of tea. They took pity on us, and that tea was the most welcome sight we had ever seen, and tasted like nectar to us ; but if ever again we visit Send and go on the river, we shall take very good care to take a tea basket.

We had a fright when we went to find our boat after tea, for it had gone ! " That's all right," said the lock-keeper, who saw our consternation. " a man has taken two little boys for a row in it." We did not think it was so very " all right," especially when twenty minutes went by and they had not returned ; but, finally, they made their appearance, and when we ventured to protest, mildly, the culprit pointed out quite logically that as the boat wasn't being used they might just as well have it, and the smallest of the two children piped up with " 'Course we can go for a ride in that boat 'cos it belongs to the man my father works for ! " In the face of such devastating arguments we could say no more, and as nothing in the boat had been touched we could hardly feel annoyed.

We had a delightful journey back to Send, and the silver ribbon was tinged with the pink of a glorious sunset as we left the river and mounted our machines, which we had parked in the front of the inn, and as we joined the procession of homebound traffic on the main road we both agreed that we had discovered one of the most delightful places near London for spending a riverside holiday. Not a very exciting place, to be sure, for the people who go down the river to dance and see life, in the sophisticated, Hampton Court manner, but ideal for anyone who wants rest and peace.

There are plenty of places on the banks of the Thames where it is possible to escape from the crowd, for instance, just past Henley there is a rough, narrow lane that leads down to a grass clearing and a boathouse. The way leading to it is not wide

FIG. 9. A PEACEFUL SPOT NEAR HENLEY

enough for anything bigger than a sidecar outfit, and even then the driver has to crouch down to avoid the trees and hedges, which almost meet overhead. Here it is possible to spend a peaceful afternoon remote from the merrymakers, and yet be able to watch the gay stream of boats on the river, and listen to the sound of ukeleles and voices harmonizing. Even the most raucous gramophone music sounds enchanting when played on the river.

There are ever so many pretty Thames-side roads. There is the one from Dachett to Bray, while one of the most beautiful roads we know is the one leading from Maidenhead down to Marlow, through the Beech woods.

CHAPTER VIII

FROCKS AND FRILLS

IT is really marvellous how clothes help or hinder Eve's capabilities. A woman will tackle almost anything provided she is suitably dressed, but put her in a ballroom in one of last year's jumpers and a soiled flannel skirt, and we guarantee that she would not be able to dance a step.

Not, of course, unless she had a colossal sense of humour or an enormous amount of cheek, but in that case she would be above the average, and we are just discussing ordinary human beings.

Put that same woman into cloth of silver, shingle her, and powder her, sheathe her feet in guinea silk stockings, and brocaded Paris shoes, give her a feather fan and an attractive partner, and she would become the very spirit of dance itself. She would sparkle and lure. She would radiate charm and beauty, even if she was usually one of the most ordinary little souls in Suburbia.

That is the influence of clothes !

It is just the same with the road girl, whether she is a driver or a passenger.

We soon discovered how important it was to be suitably dressed when motor-cycling, and we came home after our first motor-cycle ride feeling perfect frights, as well as incapable idiots, for we had gone off in our wide-brimmed hats and silk stockings. We had a sidecar machine and took it in turns to drive, but more than once we had to ask other people to start our engine for us because we were so afraid of damaging our beautiful silk stockings when giving the starter a good hefty kick, and, to crown our misery, our hats tried to blow off !

The next time we went out we took very good care to be suitably dressed, and we gradually learnt by experience what sort of clothes were the most comfortable and serviceable.

In the first place we learnt that it was not absolutely essential to wear riding breeches, and that a pair of overalls worn over a woolly skirt formed a very good substitute. On the other hand, we found it most uncomfortable to ride in skirts without the protection of the overalls, for the smartest skirt becomes bedraggled and sorry-looking after the first shower of rain, and skirts never will " stay put," but keep on blowing up, much to the wearer's discomfiture.

In very cold weather we wear riding suits made of corduroy.

Being draught-proof and almost impossible to wear out, corduroy is an ideal material for the motor-cyclist.

Our coats are made loose and knee-length, with huge poachers that will hold any amount of things without going out of shape, and the collars are made to turn down, or button up to the neck, as required. The breeches are made in the ordinary, regulation style, but they are not too tight at the knee, so that they do not become uncomfortable on a long journey.

We wear Burberry suits as a change from the corduroy. They are also excellent for hard wear, and can be cleaned and reproofed again and again, looking as good as new each time. These suits have the virtue of being very light in weight as well as weather-proof. Corduroy is rather heavy for summer wear, and we find that the others are not quite so tiring.

We have overcoats to match, of the roomy "trench-coat" pattern. These are made long enough to cover our knees when sitting on a bike, and they have plenty of fastenings, so that they are not always blowing open.

If Eve wants to look really chic on her motor-bike she will be terribly extravagant, and indulge in one of the new washable suede suits. Made of the softest skins, these suits consist of breeches, coat, and cap, and they are made in the most beautiful shades ranging from cerise to delicate rose, or from lemon to flaming orange. These all sound rather delicate shades for motor-cycling, but they are all guaranteed washable, and in any case Eve would only wear a suit of this sort on a fine summer day.

Descending from the sublime to the severely practical, a really good waterproof is very necessary. The best kind is the ordinary black rubber garment that has no fastenings in the front, but just slips on over the head, and is called a "Poncho." This rather unbecoming garment is the finest thing on the market for keeping out the rain.

The "leatherette" varieties are serviceable and cheap, and can be had in beautiful colours, while an ordinary rubber-lined "mac" has its uses, and is easy to carry on the back of the bike.

Then there is the choice of headgear. There are dozens of different types of leather helmets, but they are mostly very hot and heavy, and only suitable for very cold, wet weather. A better choice for ordinary, everyday touring would be the brightly-coloured woolly cap or the Beret. A great point is to choose a cap that is light and warm, and will not blow off, over which the wearer can adjust her goggles comfortably.

We have tried all sorts of motor-cycling footwear, from the ex-army, lace-up variety, to the ubiquitous Russian boot, and we find the latter variety as good as anything. Ours are made of a particularly strong box-calf which we have treated with

FIG. 10. COMFORT AND UTILITY IN RIDING KIT

"dubbin," and they are warm, easy to slip on, and waterproof. Being extra high in the leg, and well fitting, they look neat with breeches, and nearly reach our stocking tops.

We have lace-up pairs as well, but oh! what a time they take to lace! The girl rider should spend as much as ever she can afford on gloves. Cheap gloves are a bad investment, and she will find herself in need of a new pair in a few weeks' time.

Horschide gloves are the strongest and most waterproof, although no gloves ever made will keep out the rain unless they are given frequent waterproof treatment.

Take a large piece of household lard (as they say in the cookery books) and massage it well into the gloves, leaving them in a warm (but *not* hot!) place for a few hours, and when the lard has thoroughly soaked into the gloves give them a coating of good brown boot polish. The gloves should undergo this treatment at least once a week, and it will preserve and feed the leather, as well as making them practically waterproof. A leather coat is a precious possession, and this should also be treated kindly.

Mars oil is a good thing for leather, and ordinary Castrol " R " is another excellent leather food. Leather coats should also be left hanging in a warm place to allow the oil to soak in, and if leather is treated in this way it will never go sodden in the rain, drying stiffly and shapelessly. A good coat or pair of gloves ought to last for years.

Silk linings, worn under the gloves, will keep the hands warm in the coldest weather, for only a motor-cyclist knows how painful cold hands can be! Very early in our motor-cycling career we discovered the value of silk for warmth, and now we save all our old silk jumpers and stockings, wearing them under our woollies in the cold weather. Thus equipped, with the addition of a cosy woollen scarf, Eve can defy the most arctic weather, and always feel warm and comfortable.

CHAPTER IX

MOTOR-CYCLING AND HEALTH

MOTOR-CYCLING is not a strenuous pastime even for the delicate girl, who is not overburdened with strength and stamina. The present-day machine does not call for the powers of an Amazon, for it is so docile and easy to handle that even a schoolgirl can start and ride it with ease and safety.

A long journey on a bicycle is much more tiring than a day spent in travelling 200 miles on a motor-cycle, for in the former case the physical exertion is much greater, and the riding position is less comfortable. Here the anti-motor-cyclists might say " Yes, that is all very well, but what about the vibration and general knocking-about that one is subjected to when riding a motor-cycle! Surely that is bad for one's health!" It might have been bad twenty years ago, and we must admit that the old-fashioned machine, with its hard saddle and badly-sprung frame, was not exactly a lady's mount, but the modern machine is so well designed, and the latest types of " de luxe " saddles are so comfortable that vibration and road shocks hardly exist.

A comfortable saddle makes all the difference to the girl-rider's health and comfort, and it need not necessarily be a very elaborate or expensive one, so long as it is the right size and weight ; if she is a light weight, and the springs are too strong for her, she will be just as unhappy as if she was sitting on a saddle with no springs in it at all. All makes of saddles are supplied in different weights and sizes, and she can choose the one which best suits her.

If she has fitted on her machine a hard, cheap little saddle, and does not want to spend a great deal of money on having it changed, her best plan is to buy an air-saddle, and strap it over the existing one. These are made in the same way as the pillion seats, and they can be inflated to any required degree. They are a great aid to comfort, and cost very little.

Rubber handlebar grips will prevent any undue strain on the wrists and arms, although when a girl becomes used to riding, she will find that there is no necessity to hang on like grim death to the handlebars, but that she can steer it with the slightest touch of her fingers, and can even take her hands off the bars altogether, and still retain control of the machine.

Weather protection is just as important to health as frame and saddle comfort, and it is simply asking for trouble to start out on a long journey without being prepared for any kind of weather.

FIG. 11. MOTOR-CYCLING AS A MEANS TO HEALTH

Special Press

MOTOR-CYCLING AND HEALTH

If she is only going for a short ride, and the sun is blazing down from a brilliant blue sky, it is wise for her to strap a light raincoat on the carrier, for a summer shower will soon soak through a light frock, and it is very dangerous to ride in damp clothes.

We adopt all sorts of means to keep warm and dry in the winter. Our greatest aim and object is to keep our hands and feet warm. It is easy to wear plenty of woollies and waterproofs, but it is not so easy to protect one's hands and feet. We have never had any gloves which are absolutely waterproof; even the thick horsehide variety become sodden when riding through very heavy rain, so we fit handlebar muffs when on a winter tour. These useful accessories are made of American cloth, or other waterproof material, and they are cosily lined with fleece. They are made wide enough to fit right over the handlebars and controls, and can be adjusted in a few minutes, preventing all the misery and discomfort of riding with cold, wet hands.

We find that our old silk stockings, worn under our woollen ones keep our feet warm, but as an additional protection in very bad weather we put a thin layer of Thermogene inside our boots, or rub our feet with liniment, making them glow and tingle if they happen to get wet. A little whisky poured into damp boots will prevent a chill, if one is a long way from home, and has no change of footwear.

So long as a girl dresses suitably, and keeps warm and dry, we recommend motor-cycling as a medicine for anyone who suffers from chest complaints, and it will be found that the fresh air will soon blow away a cold in the head and strengthen lungs, while motor-cycling is a splendid cure for " nerves " and insomnia.

Naturally, as with any other kind of medicine, one must start taking the cure in small doses. It would be foolish to start with a 200 mile journey, just as it would be stupid suddenly to start taking cold baths, if accustomed to warm ones. Fifty miles a day is enough for a start, and the motor-cyclist can gradually increase her mileage until she finds that her speedometer registers quite a respectable total, and that she can undertake a long journey without feeling any sign of fatigue.

The motor-cyclist has no time for " nerves " : riding demands concentration, and she will be far too busy with the job of steering her steed to worry as to whether her nerves are out of order, while she will return home, healthily tired and full of fresh air, and will sleep soundly until the morning ; every day spent on the road will add to her health, and she will not only feel better, but it will add immeasurably to her looks.

CHAPTER X

THE ROAD GIRL'S COMPLEXION

THE average stay-at-home Eve has a most unprepossessing mental picture of the road girl. She imagines a strapping, masculine-looking creature who is a stranger to a powder-puff, wears breeches and calls people " old thing." This idea is quite wrong. The modern road girl is as careful of her appearance as her non-riding sister, and her powder puff is more important to her than her puncture repair outfit. It is not at all necessary for her to be weatherbeaten provided she takes suitable means to protect her skin against dust and wind.

These means are very simple. The first and foremost rule for the road girl when on a journey is not to use too much soap and water. The finest soap has in it a certain amount of caustic element which dries and starves the skin, robbing it of its natural oils, making it dry and coarse.

Before starting out in the morning she should thoroughly cleanse the face with cold cream, removing every vestige of dirt with a clean cloth. An application of rose or orange-flower water, lightly dabbed on the face with a piece of cotton-wool, will remove the last trace of grease, then a touch of vanishing cream and a dusting of face powder will complete a toilet that acts as a protection against the weather. At night the face should again thoroughly be cleaned with cold cream. If she must wash her face the best soap is plain, unscented Castile, as it has more oil in it, and generally it is very much purer than the highly scented kinds. A little toilet oatmeal is a good water softener, and a few drops of eau-de-Cologne in the water form a splendid tonic; but soap and water should only be used once a day, and then only in the evening, and not just before setting out.

Riding in the rain is splendid for the complexion, and will do more to clear the skin and brighten the eyes than any amount of beauty lotions.

Goggles are absolutely necessary, whether driving or riding in the sidecar. Tinted ones are the best as protection against sun glare, but even if Eve wears the best goggles in the world she is still well advised to carry with her an eye-bath and a packet of boracic powder, and to bathe her eyes every evening, using the lotion fairly strong but not too hot.

Then there is the care of the hair.

In another chapter we advise the use of woolly caps instead of

THE ROAD GIRL'S COMPLEXION

stuffy helmets. Helmets ruin the hair, although they are a great protection in case of an accident, and very warm and cosy in the winter. The woolly cap does not protect the hair from dirt, but allows plenty of ventilation, and after all, dust easily can be removed at the end of the day. Bay rum is a good cleanser, and so is eau-de-Cologne. Dip the tips of the fingers in the lotion and massage them lightly all over the scalp, then spray a little on the hair and comb with a fine-tooth comb, finishing off with a vigorous brushing with a fairly stiff brush. This treatment will remove the day's dust and keep the hair in good condition.

The road girl's hands need very special treatment, especially if she is running her own machine and does her own repair work. Here again, cold cream is her stand-by, and she must use it lavishly to keep her hands in good condition. Before starting off on a trip it is a good plan to file her finger-nails fairly short, and then dig them into the tablet of soap. This will prevent them filling with dirt, and save her much trouble with the nailbrush and orange stick when she washes her hands.

Most motor accessory people stock a preparation which can be applied to the hands before doing any dirty repair job, and makes the dirt very easy to remove. It is put up in the form of a paste, and costs about a shilling a tin. There are also several makes of motorists' soap, and these act like magic on the most hopeless-looking hands, bringing them clean in a few seconds, even if used with cold water.

Eve might think that all these precautions are rather a nuisance, but a little trouble taken at the right time will save endless misery and expense at the end of a tour. She will not have to visit a beauty parlour for an elaborate course of repair treatment, for motor-cycling will have aided, and not destroyed, her beauty. She will not have to buy her blush in a box, for on her face will bloom natural roses.

Health is the best beauty doctor, and motor-cycling is one of the best ways to health.

CHAPTER XI

THE PILLION PASSENGER

PILLION riding will always be popular unless it is actually banned by law, and it is in the hands of the pillion girl herself to make or mar her fate at the hands of the scaremongers.

There are so very many wrong ways of sitting on the "flapper bracket," and she can easily make pillion riding look uncomfortable and dangerous.

The worst offender is the one who sits coyly sideways, upsetting the balance of the machine, and forcing the driver to lean the opposite way in order to balance it. Also it is very insecure, and the passenger is quite likely to fall off when going round a bend or over a particularly bad piece of road. The usual reason for a girl having to sit sideways is that she is wearing the wrong kind of skirt, usually a short, skimpy garment which is very tight around the knees. Naturally it is impossible to ride astride in the only safe position unless she wears a skirt which has plenty of width in it.

Then there is the passenger who wriggles !

This particularly dangerous type does not get really comfortable at the start, and gives violent lurches in the middle of a particularly crowded section of Oxford Street. You just save yourself and your passenger from coming to an untimely end underneath a 'bus when she gives a mighty heave in the opposite direction, and you nearly mount the kerb. Perhaps she forgets to fasten her coat before starting, and she is busy struggling with it when you hit a pothole, she clutches you violently and nearly pushes you over the handlebars.

All those little things make for accidents, and girls are not the only offenders. Imagine having as a pillion passenger an eleven-stone man who insists on leaning down to see if the back tyre is flat ! That is the kind of thing that happens quite often, and then people shake their heads and groan about the dangers of pillion riding !

The first duty of the pillionist is to sit still ; not to try to help with the balance of the machine, but just sit astride and have faith in the driver.

Another point is to see that the back number plate is not obscured, a flapping coat may mean a £2 fine if a sharp-eyed policeman notices it, and the law is very hot on the scent of pillion faults ; also see that there are no loose ribbons or ends about you

THE PILLION PASSENGER

that might get tangled in the back wheel or driving chain, or a nasty spill might result.

Pillion footrests are essential on a long journey ; a passenger may be quite comfortable without them for the first 10 miles,

Special Press
Fig. 12. The Worst Offender is the One Who Sits Coyly Sideways

but after that the strain is felt, and one's feet and legs begin to feel as if they weigh a ton. Most firms make footrests to fit their own machines ; B.S.A.'s and several other big firms make several different types to suit various models, while the manufacturers of pillion seats usually make footrests as well.

There are any number of excellent types of pillion seats on the market, ranging in price from about 6s. The Moseley " Float on

Air " pneumatic cushion is one of the best, and it has also the virtue of being one of the cheapest. Made in several sizes to fit on any type of carrier it can be used only half inflated for a light passenger or blown up very hard for a heavy one.

The " Tansad " is another excellent and popular seat. It is a more elaborate type, very comfortable, and is made in several shapes and sizes. There are several other good makes of pillion

Topical

FIG. 13. SAFE AND COMFORTABLE

seats, including those made by the big saddle manufacturers. Some of these are luxurious, with a rail to hold on in front and a padded backrest. One of the seats shown at the Olympia Motorcycle Show last year was made like a luggage carrier. It fastened on the carrier in the usual way, but the upholstered top could be lifted up on a hinge, and there was room inside for a full change of clothing and an extra raincoat. It was a very useful accessory for a pillion tour, when luggage is always a problem. There was also a tiny mirror fitted into the lid, and it could be turned into a complete dressing-case for a camping holiday.

The seats for the carriers of sidecar outfits are very luxurious affairs. The favourite type has a circular back and armrests, which make it as comfortable as an armchair.

If in emergency the humble boating cushion is brought into

FIG. 14. NEAR THE THAMES SIDE

service, it is as well to make it a waterproof cover out of a yard of American cloth, otherwise the first shower of rain will ruin it, making it a most unpleasant thing to sit on. A few thick folds of newspaper placed underneath an ordinary cushion will help to deaden the road shocks, making it a more substantial seat. But most important of all, the cushion must be very securely fastened to the carrier with stout straps.

Give any sort of pillion seat a trial before starting on a journey of any length. It may be the wrong height, or too springy, or something else might be wrong with it, and absolutely spoil the thrill of touring " two up."

Our first attempt at taking someone on the back was very amusing. He was a very tall man, and he sat on the back of one of our machines.

Just as it was moving off, the driver rather nervous and wobbly, he stood up and allowed the rider and machine to go on without him. She churned down the road very slowly, and it was not until she had gone some distance, and was stopped in a traffic block, that she realized there was nobody on the back. Her feelings were a hectic mixture of annoyance at having been " had," and anxiety as to whether she had dropped him in the middle of the Strand.

Nowadays, we are quite used to taking people on the back, even on wet days; in fact, our machines seem to hold the road better when travelling " two up," and to suffer even less than usual from skids in grease.

Pillion luggage is a problem, and the pillion girl must first of all learn the gentle art of doing without. Haversacks are useful things, and it is remarkable how much one can stuff into capacious pockets, but it is not easy to stow away enough spare clothes for a week.

Sensible riding kit goes a long way towards solving the problem. The best costume is one that does duty for walking as well as riding. Overalls worn over a sports skirt take the place of breeches, and a Burberry raincoat will be of more practical use than a heavy leather coat that can only be worn for riding, and is much too cumbersome when off the bike. For torrential rains a rubber Poncho may be worn as an additional security.

Sensible footwear is important. Please, oh please, Miss Pillion Girl, don't wear your best champagne-coloured stockings when starting off on a ride! They may be all right in the dry weather, but if there is a shower the back of a motor-cycle is a much muddier seat than the driver's, and you will arrive home with disgraceful-looking stockings. Russian boots are the best wear for pillion riding, but failing those, a pair of dark, fairly thick golf stockings are essential for comfort and appearance.

CHAPTER XII

"TWO UP" ON TOUR

ONE of our most delightful pillion rides was a tour round Devon. We started off from London one stifling morning in the middle of August, and we were away for ten days altogether.

Our luggage consisted of two haversacks, in which we stowed all our personal luggage. At the side of the carrier we strapped a portable tent of diminutive size, for we wanted our holiday to be as cheap as possible, and it was the time of year for camping out. We used two air cushions for our pillion seat, only one of which we inflated, the other we carried underneath as a spare pillow, with a ground sheet. These formed our camping equipment.

Instead of donning riding breeches we wore woolly Sports outfits with men's seatless overalls over our skirts. This saved having to carry spare frocks for wear when we wished to appear in orthodox clothing. When we stopped anywhere and wanted to explore we merely removed the overalls and left them in the garage with our bike. We found that these overalls kept out all the rain and mud, and were also splendid for warmth. Over our light Burberrys we wore rubber "Ponchos." These rather unbeautiful garments are wonderful for keeping out the rain. It was hot and dry when we left town, but we felt that we ought to be prepared for any kind of weather.

On our heads we wore woolly caps and good Triplex goggles, while our feet were encased in stout brogues, over which fitted the "spat" tops of our overalls, forming splendid protection for our feet.

We filled our capacious pockets with all sorts of oddments which we thought we might need on the journey, until we looked exactly like Tweedledum and Tweedledee.

It is surprising how very little luggage is really necessary for a motor-cycle tour, and how very much one can do without when absolutely put to it. We were quite happy without even a pretty frock to wear in the evenings; we could, at a pinch, have carried thin voile frocks in our haversacks, but they would have been so creased that they would hardly have been worth wearing.

Being independent of trains, we chose the remotest places in which to settle for the night, and, consequently, discovered some lovely spots. If the weather looked unsettled we made tracks for a likely-looking village, and slept at a cottage, but if the night was fine we pitched our tent under the stars and slept in that, finding a friendly cottager to provide us with breakfast in the morning. Those Devonshire breakfasts were wonderful! They usually consisted of huge dishes of home-cured ham, and eggs straight from the nest, with bowls of cream and fresh raspberries or currants from the garden. This queenly feast generally cost us about 1s. 6d. each, sometimes less.

If we had tea and a bed for the night the cost was about 5s. 6d. We chose our cottages with great care, avoiding anything in the

FIG. 15

least pretentious, and it was great fun selecting exactly the right kind of place.

The nights which we spent in the open were real adventures. On one of these nights we were awakened by a cold, wet object suddenly being thrust in our faces. It was a sheep, which had found its way into our tent, and was apparently trying to tell us it was morning.

We always chose a camping place not too far away from the sea, and were able to have a glorious early morning dip. We usually had a swim in the evening, too, in order to wash away the road dust and freshen us after our travels.

We started off by way of Staines and Basingstoke, making our way over Salisbury Plain by the main road to Barnstaple. Here

"TWO UP" ON TOUR

we took to the by-roads, and tried some of the famous test hills. Our little B.S.A. made a good climb of Porlock, and we spent several hours on the top amongst the heather overlooking the thrilling blueness of the sea. Then, coasting gently down Countisbury we put up for the night just outside Lynmouth. It looked rather like rain, so we found quarters indoors, but did not choose a place right in Lynmouth itself, as it seemed much too popular a village to be particularly cheap.

In the morning we explored, and, finally, climbed Lynton hill,

Photo Press

FIG. 16. WE TAKE PONCHO FOR A RIDE

and went up the hill that overlooks Watersmeet, an exquisite beauty spot on the top of the world. We even tried the fearsome hill known as Beggar's Roost, this was asking a lot of a little $2\frac{1}{4}$ horse-power machine with two eight-stone passengers aboard, but we had a very low bottom gear, and just managed it with not an ounce of power to spare.

Turning to the right at the top of Beggar's Roost we took an extremely bumpy road through Simonsbath to the Moors, pitching our tent among the heather, and feeling glad that it was not necessary to average any great speed on the rough Devon lanes. The next day we slid down an alarming hill into the diminutive village of Exford. Here we felt exactly as if we had stepped out of real life and on to the stage in the middle of the village scene in a pantomime. The bright red cottages, with their fuchsia bushes and rose trees, looked as if they were painted on a background of vivid blue, the village green was absolutely made for a beauty chorus to prance on and sing an opening song, while surely Dick Whittington and his mother lived in the little inn, with its latticed windows and picturesque porch.

We had a typical Devon breakfast in Dick Whittington's house, which was just as delightful inside, and made our way to Minehead, where we had a bathe. Then, with our wet bathing costumes wound round our handlebars, we took the main road to Bridgwater, but somehow we turned down the wrong road and got lost, arriving at Bampton instead, where we had a sort of tea-lunch. Near Wiveliscombe we found another charming village called Waterow, right on the main road, where we stayed for the night at a cottage which had a garden built on the hill. Our bedroom overlooked the almost perpendicular lawn where hens and ducks wandered at will. It looked for all the world like a nursery wallpaper.

We returned via Bristol and Bath, visiting Cheddar Gorge *en route*, and taking two days over the journey. It was agreed that we had discovered an ideal way of spending a holiday, both from the health and economy point of view. The cost of the whole week was something like £2 each. Our little machine gave us no trouble, and we had only one puncture. We took it in turns to drive, and made it a rule always to stop at the end of every 20 miles just to stretch our legs and have a rest, always remembering that it was a holiday, and that it did not matter if we only did 40 miles a day, consequently, we were quite fit and fresh each evening, and ready to put our bike away for the night and enjoy a walk or a bathe. Our mileage for the week was between eight and nine hundred miles from the time we left home until we returned.

CHAPTER XIII

THE "SOLO" RIDER

THE time may come when Eve tires of sitting in a sidecar, or on a pillion seat, and longs to have a machine of her own.

She may have been used to hanging on by her eyebrows to the belt of a super-speed maniac who scorns to ride anything capable of less than 90 miles per hour, but she will find that it is a very different feeling to have complete control of her own machine. When she has finally decided to " paddle her own canoe," so to speak, she must observe one golden rule for beginners, and *start with something small.* A $2\frac{1}{4}$ horse-power machine is quite powerful enough for a lady rider's first " solo " mount.

Our own debut on a solo motor-cycle was made under difficulties. We borrowed from a motor-cycling friend a rusty-looking, spidery object that was more like a petrolized bicycle than a real, self-respecting motor-cycle. It had no spring forks, a hard, bony little saddle, and bicycle-sized wheels. The engine was the only good thing about it, and this was almost too good for a beginner, for it sprinted off at about 20 miles an hour.

On this masterpiece of engineering we took our first lessons in solo riding, and to this day we marvel at the fact that we are still alive to tell the tale, for our initial effort was to take it in turns to ride round and round a busy Bloomsbury square.

There was no clutch or kick-starter, and the engine roared into life by means of violent pedalling. Our chief trouble was trying to pluck up enough courage to stop, for the saddle was too high to allow us to put our feet to the ground, and our efforts to dismount were not exactly the picture of grace.

After many trials and tribulations, eventually we became proficient on our primitive steed, and we could even mount and dismount without damaging ourselves or the machine.

Our next effort was on a motor-cycle whose engine was driven on the friction-drive principle. Unfortunately, the designer had forgotten that sometimes in England it rains, and had left the friction disc exposed, so that when it became wet it refused to grip; consequently, the engine would work very hard without giving much result. Sometimes oil, as well as water, would find its way on to the disc, and we dared not move far away from home without taking with us packets of fuller's earth or resin, with which to sprinkle the friction drive.

The method of starting was acrobatic in the extreme. We

would run alongside the machine for all we were worth, and when the engine fired we kicked the foot-clutch. (The clutch was worked by a sort of brake-pedal arrangement.) Sometimes we managed to disengage the clutch and bring the machine to a standstill with the engine running, according to schedule, sometimes we jabbed our ankle on a sharp bit of the frame, but usually we failed altogether in our efforts to stop the bike, and it would go on without us.

Its chief virtues lay in the facts that it was not powerful enough to do any harm, and that it had a comfortable riding position.

This quaint machine saw quite a lot of service, and when we had become expert in performing the various antics which were necessary, we became quite fond of it, although its maximum speed was not more than about 20 miles an hour, and its lack of acceleration was sometimes embarrassing, especially when the polite driver of a coalcart or a lorry would wave it on, and the poor little thing simply *couldn't* muster up enough speed to get in front. We had this machine for several months, and then we were given the chance of buying two second-hand Ner-a-cars, so we sold our old love for £4.

Our Ner-a-cars were elegant machines, and even Aunt Julia had to admit that they were ideal mounts for ladies, with their all-enclosed engines and comfortable riding position.

We liked their efficient mudguarding and general cleanliness, and we could even ride on them to the tennis court, dressed in immaculate white, and arrive there without soiling our shoes and stockings.

They had $2\frac{1}{2}$ horse-power two-stroke engines, and, curiously enough, these were also built on the friction-drive principle, but there the similarity to our other mount ended, for in these the designer had succeeded where the other failed, and the engines of the Ner-a-cars were smooth-running, with a good turn of speed.

One machine was much faster than the other, and we nicknamed the slower one of the two " The Old Lady." Her road performance was good, but she wouldn't be hurried, and her engine was so quiet and genteel that, when waiting in a traffic block, one had to lean down and listen to hear whether she was still " ticking over."

The other machine was much more dashing, and would spring along merrily while The Old Lady would potter along gently behind.

She suffered from a slight cough in her carburettor, but she was quite dependable, and although she was often late, she was never absent, and always gave very good service.

We had these machines for over a year, during which time we gained a great deal of useful road experience, doing some very

FIG. 17. HILLS HAVE NO TERRORS FOR A MODERN MACHINE

Fox Photos

long journeys on them, including a trip to Scotland and back, when we travelled a thousand miles in less than a week, and an eight-day's tour round the South Coast.

At the end of the year our total mileage was rather more than 8,000 miles, and we sometimes did as much as 200 miles in a day.

We felt sorry to part with our Ner-a-cars, but eventually we grew tired of the fussiness of the two-stroke, and wanted to try four-strokes for a change, so we sold them for quite a good price (for we had taken care of them, and they were still in good condition), and started looking round for something fresh.

We held many consultations with various motor-cycling friends, all of whom recommended entirely different machines, and sang the praises of their own particular mount, and after a great deal of arguing we decided on Baby B.S.A.'s.

We chose " de Luxe " models, and took delivery early in the year. They were gentlemanly, good-tempered little fellows, and although we felt rather strange on them at first (for they were quite different to our Ner-a-cars, both in steering and balance), we soon became accustomed to them, and we have now been riding Baby B.S.A.'s for the last two years.

CHAPTER XIV

LEARNING TO RIDE

In a previous chapter we gave a lurid description of our own experiences when learning to ride a solo machine, but these need not alarm the would-be lady rider, for she will not have to face any of these difficulties when she first mounts a modern " de Luxe " model. We will assume that she has chosen her machine, but if she has never ridden a motor-cycle before, it would be as well for her to arrange to have a " trial run " before purchasing.

Most motor-cycle agents are very obliging about arranging a trial for their customers, and with the new rider it takes the form of a lesson, while if she chooses her mount at Olympia, she will find on every stand demonstrators who are willing and anxious to teach her to ride, for most motor-cycle firms want to encourage lady riders, and give them all the help they can.

At last year's show we played the parts of demonstrators and general advisors to girl riders, and made a speciality of teaching the novice to ride. One of us would take out an intending purchaser on the back of a machine, and having selected a quiet street we would let her take the handlebars and try for herself. It was not easy to find a quiet spot near Olympia during Show Week, but if it was very crowded and busy we used to take our pupil as far as Barnes Common.

We began the lesson by explaining the controls, and made her learn by heart the position of the petrol and air levers, the clutch and brake controls, and the various positions of the gears.

We would also make quite certain that she could ride a " push bike." It was surprising how many people thought they could ride a motor-cycle although they had not even gained a sense of balance through riding an ordinary bicycle.

For the first attempt we would start up the engine for her, and then, when she had mounted, we would run alongside while she put it into first gear and let in the clutch. Most of our pupils would glide off beautifully at the first attempt, but a few of them had to try several times before they made a successful " getaway." They would stop the engine, or start with such a jerk that they would become alarmed and open the throttle too widely, and if it was not for our restraining hand on the back carrier the machine would have careered off at 30 miles an hour.

If we were teaching someone who was very timid we would take her to the top of a gentle slope and persuade her to coast down the hill with the engine shut off and the machine in neutral. This gave her confidence, and would teach her the use of her brakes, and how easy it was to pull up and put her feet to the ground.

We would then set her the task of starting up. We found that the easiest way for her to learn was to put the machine on the stand, or lean it against the kerb. It is just a little difficult at first to remember to drop the exhaust lever and depress the kick-starter at exactly the right moment, but it is only a knack, and needs no actual physical strength. Ten minutes practice is usually enough for a girl to be able to start her motor-bike at the

FIG. 18. THE NEW BABY B.S.A.
A GOOD MAKE OF MINIATURE MACHINE

very first kick. Most people were very quick to learn, and about half-an-hour's tuition was all they required.

Most of our pupils were quite young, but we had a sprinkling of elderly women.

Early one morning a handsome, grey-haired woman came on to the stand. She was beautifully dressed and very dignified, and did not look at all like a would-be motor-cyclist, but to our surprise she explained that her daughter owned a motor-cycle and was very fond of riding, and that she was always trying to persuade her mother to come out on the carrier. " I tried it once," she said, " and I did not like it, any more than I like riding in a sidecar, and I think I would much prefer to ride a machine of my own. I've had a lesson on my daughter's Norton, but I think it is rather high-powered for me, and I want to try one of your $2\frac{1}{4}$ ' de Luxe ' models." This surprising mother of a motor-cycling daughter overcame her objections to pillion riding sufficiently to accompany us to our favourite spot on Barnes Common,

LEARNING TO RIDE

Fig. 19. Mrs. Grenfel on the Francis Barnett

Fig. 20. A Neat "Zenith" Miniature

Two Good Makes of Miniature Machines

and here she took complete command of the bike, handling it as if she had been used to riding all her life. We explained the controls to her, and she rode off, being away so long that we grew quite anxious about her, but just as we were contemplating going in search of her, on the other machine, she returned, quite calm and collected, and very pleased with the little lightweight's performance. " It'll do fifty ! " she said delightedly, " just as you said it would." We took her back to Hammersmith, and the very next day she put in her order with the local agent.

Another lady past her first youth explained that she was going to take up motor-cycling because she was lonely, and she wanted to become a member of a motor-cycling club and meet new people. In fact, all sorts of unlikely people were numbered among the " inquiries " during the Show.

Men chose motor-cycles for their daughters, and their wives chose them for themselves, and most of the women showed an intelligent interest in the working of a motor-cycle, paying more attention to gear ratios and engine capacity than to the colour of the tank. There were, certainly, a few simple souls who asked silly questions, for instance, one day we watched a lady walk all round the A.J.S. stand and carefully examine all the models, peering near-sightedly at their tanks, then she came over to the B.S.A. stand and did the same thing, finally, she approached one of the assistants and said " Can I have painted on the tank any initials I like ? "

Another fair inquirer wanted to know if she could have her motor-cycle enamelled pale blue, instead of the standard colour, as blue was her lucky colour, and whether it would cost any more ! She was most disappointed when she found that no motor-cycle firm could supply her with a pale blue bicycle at ordinary black-and-gold price.

Luckily, as we say, these peculiar inquiries were in the minority, and it was quite a simple business to attend to most of the lady riders. Several girls of the Eton-cropped, tomboy type showed an interest in the high-powered models, and wanted to know which one was the fastest, and what was its maximum speed, but most of the feminine interest centred around the " Baby," and most women were more concerned about a motor-cycle's reliability and cleanliness than its maximum speed.

CHAPTER XV

ON CHOOSING A MOUNT

EVEN after several years of " solo " riding we still find that a 2¼ horse-power machine is quite powerful enough for ordinary, everyday use, and so far we have not succumbed to the temptation of buying something bigger, although we must confess that there is a certain fascination in sitting astride a powerful speed-iron that possesses enough horse-power to pull a four-seater car, and will do 50 miles an hour on half-throttle.

A 2¼ horse-power motor-cycle is very cheap to run, and the initial cost of it is not much more than the amount the average business girl would spend in a year in train fares.

It is very economical with petrol, being capable of anything from a hundred to a hundred and twenty miles to the gallon, while its oil consumption is about a thousand miles to a quart.

It has the virtue of not running the owner into debt at the garage, for the lightweight machine is small enough to wheel through the passage and store in the back yard. If there is not a convenient shed, then a waterproof sheet can be bought for a few shillings, and this will protect it from the weather. Garage bills mount up alarmingly, and do so add to the cost of upkeep, so it is a good idea to avoid them altogether, except for occasional repairs. In London they charge as much as a shilling per night for a small machine, while in the provinces they are almost as bad. After a great deal of trouble we did find a garage that only charged us 3s. 6d. each per week for garaging our B.S.A.'s, but these were very special terms.

Another point in favour of the small machine is its handiness in traffic. The low-riding position enables her to put both her feet down when waiting in a traffic block, and its light weight and general controllability make it possible to wheel it into the kerb if she happens to stop her engine, and has not quite recovered from her beginner's clumsiness in starting up.

Ease of starting is essential in a lady's machine, for no girl wants to wear out her strength and her temper in kicking-over an obstinate engine. Most of the small machines are very easy to start, and on our own bikes the engine usually roars into life at the first kick.

Cleanliness is important; an ill-mannered motor-cycle that spatters oil on the rider and whose mudguarding is scanty, will never win the favour of a lady, even if she wears her oldest clothes and does not care in the least about her appearance. She will soon lose her zest for riding if she is constantly being treated to a bath of mud and oil, thrown up from the road and the engine.

Although several firms make special open-framed ladies' models, they are not really necessary, and we prefer the ordinary standard type with an extra low-riding position and semi-sporting bars. Most of the former seem to have a top-heavy, "cut-in-halves" appearance. The Scott is an open-framed machine, but it is in a class by itself, and a perfect machine of its kind. For the girl who has had some riding experience, and who wants a safe, speedy motor-cycle, which is ideally clean and comfortable, and who is willing to pay a good price, we recommend a Scott. It is one of the nearest approaches to The Ideal Motor-Cycle in the three-fifty class.

A.J.S., Ariel, Triumph, Enfield, Raleigh, B.S.A. and others make baby machines suitable for the beginner. They all cost thirty to thirty-five guineas, and are all reliable and simple to ride. The "de Luxe" models are usually fitted with a three-speed gear box, clutch, and kick starter, and have fitted as standard a really comfortable saddle, usually a "Terry" or a "Brooks."

Our own small machines are capable of 50 miles an hour, but they will tick over smoothly in top gear at 10 miles an hour if necessary; they are excellent machines on which to learn to ride, for their gear boxes are practically fool-proof, and even if the novice occasionally makes terrible noises when changing up or down it need not be a cause for alarm, for it will do no serious damage, and she will soon get into the way of changing quietly.

The Francis Barnett deserves special mention among the two-stroke family. It is even tinier than the $2\frac{1}{4}$ four-strokes, for its power unit is only $1\frac{3}{4}$ horse-power, and yet it is capable of doing quite a lot of hard work. A friend of ours owns one, and she travels all over the country, and her daily work makes it essential for her to do at least 40 miles a day, and sometimes much more. She looks the picture of health, for she rides in all weathers, and we have never heard her complain of engine trouble.

Another good, trouble-free two-stroke is the Velocette, but this is just a little higher-powered than the Francis Barnett, and rather more expensive.

The E.W. Douglas is one of the best of the twin-cylinder machines. The even torque of a "twin" makes it remarkably steady and smooth running, and it is almost impossible when riding an E.W. to have a side-slip in greasy weather. Most of the weight of an E.W. is below the hubs, and this makes it very comfortable and safe to handle on rough roads or in traffic. It is a little more powerful than the "Baby" machines, being $2\frac{3}{4}$ horse-power, but its good design makes it quite safe for a beginner,

ON CHOOSING A MOUNT

and it is really amazingly cheap in price. Even a $2\frac{3}{4}$ machine is handy enough to keep in the back yard, and it does not cost much more in upkeep than its little brother. The tax is £2 a year instead of 30s., and it is not quite so good on petrol, but these are the only two material differences, when once the rider has overcome the initial cost.

That useful institution, the instalment plan, is in force with most big motor-cycle manufacturers, and one can take delivery

Fox Photos

FIG. 21. A $2\frac{1}{4}$ H.P. MACHINE IS QUITE POWERFUL FOR ORDINARY EVERYDAY USE

of a machine on payment of a small deposit and a sum every month, and they will also arrange about insurance. It is very important for the motor-cyclist to be insured. She has not only to guard against her own carelessness or bad luck on the road, but she also has to take into consideration the fact that there might be other novices in charge of cars and motor-cycles, and she must insure herself against "third party" as well as her own risks. It is false economy for a rider to save money on an insurance policy, however careful she might be.

It is a good idea for the intending girl rider to make her final choice of a mount at the Motor-Cycle Show which is held each

Autumn at Olympia. Here she will meet other lady riders, and be able to compare notes with them, and here she will be able to make a tour of the stands, trying riding positions and comparing prices, until, finally, she has discovered the very thing she wants, at just the right price to suit her purse.

The 1927 Olympia Show marks the advent of several new "Babies." B.S.A.'s have made a tiny two-speed two-stroke which sells for twenty-eight guineas, while the new 172 c.c. Zenith is one of the neatest of the newcomers, and ought to be very popular amongst new lady riders.

The 1927 500 c.c. Rudge is in marked contrast to these midgets, but although it is a large, high-powered machine, the low-riding position and coupled brakes make it a safe and easy mount to handle, and it will take one of the first places amongst the motor-cycle aristocracy.

CHAPTER XVI

THE NEW MACHINE

EVE has unwound the wrappings from her new machine, and as it stands there in all its shining splendour, she must be prepared to spend several hours on it before it is actually ready for her to ride. The engine will have been " run in " on the bench in the factory, and it will have had a road test of about 50 miles before leaving the works, but she will find that she will be able to make plenty of adjustments that will materially add to her comfort and happiness on the road.

Her first care must be to adjust the saddle and footrests, and experiment with different positions until she finds the one that best suits her. A saddle that is too high, or footrests that are too far back, or too far forward, will spoil her enjoyment of motor-cycling, and she will return from her first journey feeling tired and unhappy. Having discovered the ideal riding position she should next go over all the nuts and bolts with a large spanner, to see that nothing has shaken loose in transit, and also see that there is plenty of grease in the gear-box, and that the forks and wheel-hubs have been well lubricated, and use the oil can or grease gun freely on any dry-looking spots. She can then fill up with oil and petrol, and start off on her first journey. If she experiences any difficulty in starting the engine, a slight adjustment of the plug points may make things easier, as they might be too far apart, or perhaps the new engine is just a little stiff, but this newness will soon wear off, and in any case the new rider will find no difficulty in securing obliging helpers, who will kick-start the machine for her.

She must take care to give her machine plenty of oil. There is no such thing as over-oiling a new engine, and it is far better to oil up the plug than to damage the bearings through under-oiling. For the first 200 miles a steady stream of thin, blue smoke should issue from the exhaust pipe after that; the supply can be cut down considerably, and a slight vapour is sufficient indication that the machine is getting its proper quantity of oil.

The oiling system on our first solo machine was very simple, in fact, it was one of the few easy things to manage on that particular bicycle, for we just mixed the oil with the petrol, and our only difficulty was to discover exactly the right proportions. We found the Castrol X.L. was the best kind for this " petroil " system of lubrication, and that the engine liked half a pint in every gallon of petrol.

Most of the " de Luxe " models are fitted with very efficient systems of mechanical oiling. One just turns the indicator until the exhaust pipe shows that the supply is correct, and then leaves it at that. Our own machines have a hand-pump, as well as mechanical oiling, and when they were brand-new we gave them one whole turn of the indicator, and a pumpful every 10 or 12 miles and then, when the engines were properly run in, we cut down the supply to less than half this quantity. It is not good economy to buy cheap oil, and it will be cheaper in the long run for the motor-cyclist to use in her little mount the best and finest oil obtainable, for the engine will need far less overhauling, and will last much longer without being decarbonized than if she fed it on any old oil at any old price. It is as well, also, for her to always feed it on the same brand, for the baby engine cannot digest a mixture of different oils, any more than a human baby can digest a mixture of different patent foods, and she will soon become disordered and peevish if she starts suffering from oiling trouble. Most clutches are made, nowadays, with Ferodo insets, and they are sufficiently strong to stand any amount of hard wear, but even so, it is as well for the beginner to start in the right manner by learning to use her gears. She can slip the clutch a little, in traffic, to keep up the revs. of the engine, and ensure smooth running, but she should not do it too much, and she should never strain a new engine by keeping in top gear when climbing a steep hill, or when taking an acute bend. Gear changing on a motor-cycle is much easier than in a car, and can be mastered in a few minutes, but the principle of gear changing in a car and on a bike is the same, and the gears should be persuaded, and not forced.

We rode our machines for several hundred miles before we opened the tool bags, and then, when we did have occasion to use a spanner, it was only to see that none of the nuts and bolts had worked loose, and to tighten up the driving chains, which had stretched slightly.

We had our first involuntary stop when we had been riding about two months, and our speedometers indicated between eight and nine hundred miles. We were on our way up North, when one of our bicycles started to miss fire, and slow up, and, finally, it stopped altogether. We were very raw, and knew nothing about troubles on the road, but we tested the plug and looked forlornly at the magneto, and then we did the obvious thing, and tried to flood the carburettor, and finding that it was getting no petrol, although there was plenty in the tank, we examined the float chamber and petrol pipe, and removed quite a lot of chips of green enamel, while the carburettor looked as if someone had been making tea in it.

THE NEW MACHINE

This is a usual trouble with a new machine. The tank may be slightly dusty when it leaves the works, and the grime and dust finally finds its way into the carburettor. It is as well, on this account, to take the petrol pipe off and rinse out a new tank with petrol before filling up. This was our only " spot of trouble," and this only happened to one machine. At the end of a thousand miles running we had both machines completely overhauled by the local agents, just to make sure that the engines were in good condition, but after the first decarbonization, a $2\frac{1}{4}$ machine will run for three times as many miles without further attention.

CHAPTER XVII

REPAIRS, REPLACEMENTS, AND ACCESSORIES

VERY few girls are born with a love of things mechanical, and, unlike her brother, Eve seldom has a burning desire to examine the inside of an engine, in order to find out what makes it " go."

A mere man will feel soul-satisfying rapture in the contemplation of a good-looking boiler, but the feminine mind has not acquired this taste for mechanical beauty, and usually would prefer to examine the creations in a milliner's window, or the interior of a confectioner's shop. Not feeling particularly interested, the average girl rider finds it difficult to learn anything about the inside of her motor-cycle's engine, and repair jobs, which are a joy to the mechanically minded, become hard work to her.

Naturally, there are exceptions, and we know several girls who are never so happy as when they are sitting on the floor of the garage absorbed in dissecting a carburettor. Some will take to pieces their machine, just for the sheer joy of putting it together, and what is even more remarkable, they manage the putting-together process without having any extra bits left over, but these girls are exceptions, and the great majority prefer to leave the important overhauling in the capable hands of the big brother.

Nevertheless, in order to save constant small repair bills, she ought to learn how to effect her own minor repairs, for the big brother is not always on hand, and she will find the knowledge very useful when on the road alone, and miles away from anywhere. Before starting out she should see that her tool bag contains other things besides a powder puff and a bar of chocolate.

The tool kit should consist of an adjustable spanner, two or three set spanners that actually *fit* the nuts on the bike, a box spanner to use in case a wheel has to be removed, a pair of pliers, tyre levers, screwdriver, a little " nest " of magneto tools, some copper wire, a spare plug, some extra chain links, a valve spring, and some spare tyre valves, and, most important of all, an adequate puncture outfit and a spare inner tube.

The puncture fiend is the chief cause of stoppages on the road. Although motor-cycles have been brought to such a state of perfection, no one has managed to invent a puncture-proof tyre. There are preparations which can be pumped into the tyre to prevent small punctures, but they are not very satisfactory, and tyres are still the weakest part of the modern motor-cycle.

In the unlucky event of a puncture, always make an effort to

REPAIRS, REPLACEMENTS AND ACCESSORIES 63

find the spot before removing the tyre, and also look for signs of a faulty valve ; for by making a thorough examination, she may obviate the unpleasant necessity of removing the wheel.

She ought to practise at home the art of removing a wheel and taking off a tyre, for although she will usually find on the road plenty of nice people ready to help her, it is as well to know how to do it herself, and to know all about the brake and chain adjustments. The method of locating an elusive puncture is to inflate

Fox Photos

Fig. 22. Many Hands Make Light Work

the tube and immerse it in water, the bubbles will then indicate its whereabouts. Having discovered it, thoroughly dry the tube and clean it before applying the solution, which should be left until it is in a tacky state before adjusting the patch. Leave the patch to dry before replacing the tyre.

When on the road she is hardly likely to have any serious engine trouble, but she should know enough about her machine to detect such small faults as a choked jet, or a dirty or oily plug. She will soon learn by the sound of the engine whether her mount is in good health, or if it needs attention.

A teaspoonful of oil mixed with the petrol will cure a squeaky valve. The brake, clutch, and chain adjustments are usually very simple, and it is very little trouble for her to do these herself, while it is the work of a few moments to " run over " her mount with a spanner, and make sure that all the nuts and bolts are secure.

The oil can and grease gun ought to be used every 500 miles, and the chains should be cleaned as well as greased, otherwise the dirt and grit that collect on them will soon cause them to wear. She may never need to replace a valve spring, but it is as well for her to learn how to do it, and to carry with her a small valve lifter just in case she needs it.

During the first two years she ought not to need any replacements except an occasional clean plug, and even then her only serious purchase will be a set of new tyres. The average life of a motor-cycle tyre is between fifteen and twenty thousand miles, and it is always as well to buy the best tyres she can, and not try to economize by buying cheap ones.

Some girl riders delight in " gadgets," and there is no end to the list of accessories, useful and otherwise, which she can fit on to her machine. The useful articles include legshields, handlebar screens and mirrors, a neat spare tube carrier which fits on to one of the back-carrier stays and looks rather like a man's collarbox, and an infinite variety of extra toolbags and luggage carriers.

A speedometer would make a handsome present to a motorcyclist. It is not a necessity, unless she is a Trials rider, but it is a good companion on a long journey, and it is fascinating to watch it tell the tale of the miles.

We have small, but efficient, legshields to fit during winter months: they protect our legs from mud and rain, and help to keep our feet warm and dry. We also have neat little Easting wind-screens which act as splendid weather protection.

These keep-you-clean gadgets are very useful to the business girl who wishes to use her bike for going to and from the office, and for the girl who rides to the golf course and tennis court.

CHAPTER XVIII

ROAD SENSE

NOT so very long ago there was an outcry in the Press against the girl motorist. If a lady driver of a car or motor-cycle had an accident, the papers devoted half columns to the event, and deplored the average woman's lack of road sense. All this was very unfair, for statistics prove that women are just as cautious as men, but it has given the lady driver something to live down, and it is as well for the beginner to start her road-faring career by being very careful to avoid accidents, and always being particularly courteous to other people on the road.

Road sense is a mixture of imagination and concentration, and enables a motorist to know what a driver in front is going to do before he actually does it. A driver who has plenty of road sense never leaves anything to chance. If she uses her imagination she will realize that the person in front is quite likely to make mistakes, and she will always be prepared for them doing the wrong thing. They may not give a signal, but she must be ready for them making a sudden turn to right or left at a cross-road, and never be going too fast to be unable to pull up in her own length. When crossing a road she should not be content with sounding her horn, but her imagination should tell her that other people might be crossing at the same time.

It does not require much imagination in order to follow the road signs and signals, but it does require a certain amount of powers of observation and common sense, and this is where concentration becomes necessary. The road user has a definite responsibility, and she must keep her mind on the job all the time.

A white line is painted on the corner of a road for a purpose, and if she keeps to her own side of it she is quite safe, but even then she should always be driving slowly enough to be able to avoid anyone going in the opposite direction.

It is always as well to keep within the ten-miles-an-hour limit whenever she sees displayed the familiar circular sign, on entering a village. The villagers consider that the sign is quite sufficient protection, and they have a habit of crossing the road suddenly, without giving a thought to passing traffic, while the village constable is sometimes on the look-out for motorists who are in too much of a hurry, and she may have to pay a return visit to that particular village, in order to attend the local police court.

The "Steep Hill" sign is another to which she must pay

particular attention. If she has never been on that particular road before, and has no idea of the gradient of the hill, it is a wise move for her to engage low gear before descending, especially if the road is greasy. A violently applied brake will sometimes result in a bad skid, and the engine will act as a natural brake. There is a special chapter devoted to Trials riding, in which we have dealt very thoroughly with the art of riding on bad roads, so there is no need to dwell on the subject in this chapter, which deals with main-road riding.

To the alert driver, who has cultivated the power of concentration, many trifling objects act as natural road signs, and instinctively suggest danger. A ball or hoop rolling across the road immediately warns the driver of the presence of children, or the top of a car or the end of a riding whip seen over the top of a hedge will warn her of the presence of a hidden side-road.

The training process will not take very long, and the girl rider will soon find that she does the right thing by instinct, and that she has even developed an almost uncanny habit of knowing just when the pedestrian in front intends stepping out in front of her wheel, or when she has to slow up in order to avoid an obstruction round the corner.

There have been published any amount of textbooks on " Road Sense " and " Safety First," but she can gain more knowledge from practical experience than she ever will from books, and a little practice will soon enable her to read road conditions, and so learn to anticipate danger and act correctly.

If the beginner is a Londoner, she will not find it very easy to avoid traffic, and she must cultivate a traffic sense, as well as a road sense.

To the girl who is new to motor-cycling, the idea of steering a bike through London traffic is rather terrifying, but it is really much easier than it looks.

The London streets are very busy, but all the traffic is so well organized that it is only necessary for her to be able to keep her place in the procession, to stop in a traffic block and start off again without stopping her engine, and to pay particular attention to the meaning of the policeman's signal. Even if, at first, she does break the traffic rules, the London policeman is a very sympathetic type, and she will probably escape with nothing worse than a scolding, but she must make a point of at once learning the " don'ts " that form the traffic rules. For instance, DON'T ride the wrong side of an island, DON'T ride on the wrong side of the road, DON'T try to squeeze past a bus on the near side, and DON'T cross the road without putting out a hand in plenty of time to warn the people behind, and not only that, but see that everyone behind has seen your signal, and that there

ROAD SENSE

is not someone coming blindly on without any regard for their own safety or yours. People do sometimes act in a most foolhardy fashion in the busiest streets, and one must always be on the alert.

When one is used to it, it is really pleasanter to ride in London than in any of the busy provincial towns, and much simpler, for the policeman's signals are so easy to understand, and everything is so well organized.

The " Merry-go-round " system which is now in force in all the busy traffic centres is rather confusing to the newcomer to London traffic, but the Londoner has soon become quite used to going round the whole of Trafalgar Square in order to reach his own particular turning, and now welcomes it as a great time-saving scheme. It is much better for the nerves and temper to go a little out of one's way than to wait for, perhaps, a quarter of an hour in a traffic block, as one used to do.

CHAPTER XIX

THE LAW AND THE LADY RIDER

SOMETIMES the arm of the law is raised for more sinister purposes than merely to hold up the traffic, and however kindly-disposed a policeman might feel towards the lady rider he must do his duty, and sometimes treat the girl offender as harshly as he treats her big brother.

The speed-trap is the chief plague of the motor-cyclist, and the chief delight of the police force.

There is nothing more thrilling than to ride along a stretch of good main road, where one can see for miles ahead, and feel the machine leap forward as one opens wide the throttle, but it is on these innocent-looking stretches that the speed-trap usually operates.

That is why speed-traps are rather unfair, for there may be no turnings or cross-roads for a mile ahead, in fact, nothing to make " speeding " dangerous on that particular section of road, and yet people are allowed to do 45 miles an hour across a dangerous cross-road and escape scot-free, unless there is actually an accident. Until the speed-limit is removed, and replaced with safety-first methods, the speed-trap will flourish, and continue to bring in revenue to the local councils.

The motor-cyclist must keep open a wary eye for these traps, for they are not always easy to recognize. If she sees a harmless-looking individual sitting on the side of the road with a bicycle beside him, let her beware, and slow down for the next mile to the legal limit of 20 miles an hour.

Sometimes the men operating the " trap " wear uniform, and then it is easy to recognize it, but more often than not the speed of a vehicle is timed along the " Straight Mile " by men in plain clothes, and a third man in uniform is there, just ahead of the actual " trap," to undertake the legal formalities, for plain-clothes men have not the power to charge anybody.

Sometimes they adopt the comic-postcard method of hiding behind a hedge, but this is rather out of date.

In some places they have a motor-cycle police corps. Two policemen in charge of a sidecar combination chase the offender, and having caught him they proceed with the charge.

We have actually only paid one visit to Court, and that was to answer to a charge of speeding.

It happened on our way home from Brooklands, the two of us, on our B.S.A.'s, and two others, whom, for the sake of the story, we will call Jim and Bill, riding two solo Triumphs.

THE LAW AND THE LADY RIDER

We were full of the joy of the road and an anxiety to get home, for Bill had invited us all to his house to tea, and we were speeding along the beautiful switchback road known as the Cobham Straight Mile, that leads on to the main Guildford Road, when we fell bang into the arms of the law, represented by a large policeman who had stepped out from behind a telegraph post and was waiting in the middle of the road.

He was joined almost immediately by the "trap," which consisted of two plain-clothes men on bicycles. One of them pointed to his watch. "You were doing 45 miles an hour, missie," he said to one of us. "This is your fault for asking us to tea, Bill," was Jimmy's ungrateful remark as he drew alongside. The man in blue started writing in his little black book. "Hanything you say will be taken down and used in Hevidence Hagainst you," he said, licking the point of his pencil. "Licences, please." Luckily we were all able to produce them. "What's this?" he said, crossly, as he tried to decipher the various scrawls on the back of Bill's licence, "Meet Mama, three-thirty." "Don't you know, young man, that these 'ere pages are for hendorsements honly, and not to be used for making notes of happointments." Bill murmured something that sounded like an apology, and whispered hoarsely to us, "Meet Mama isn't an appointment, it's the name of a horse!"

After further formalities and much scratching in the notebook we were allowed to depart with the information that a summons would be served on each of us in due course.

We duly received our invitations to Court, and appeared at the County "Assizes" to answer to our charge of exceeding the legal speed-limit. The court was crowded with all types of humanity, from vagrant gipsies to city men in silk hats, but the law had levelled us all, and leather-coated motorists rubbed shoulders with tramps and beggars, as we all sat in rows on the hard benches.

Quite three-quarters of the people were there on motoring charges, and were fined anything from 10s. to £5 for their various offences. The speed fines were worked out on a sliding scale, it cost £3 to exceed 35 miles an hour, and £4 to do over 40, whilst a failure to produce one's licence cost another pound. Speed was dear, but noise was comparatively cheap, for the owners of machines that were not fitted with efficient silencers were only fined 15s.

Bill was the first of the four of us to be called, and he looked rather frightened as he faced the magistrate, but it cheered us all considerably when we heard the policeman read from his little black book the important statements which he had taken down "in hevidence hagainst him." "When I stopped him, defendant said, 'That's your fault for inviting us to tea, Jimmie,'" he read, and a guffaw from all of us brought a look of reproof to the face of the magistrate.

We were all fined £4 each, and we returned home feeling that "speeding" in that particular territory was a very expensive luxury.

We have had several other escapes from answering to other charges. When riding "pillion" we have, with tears and pleadings, managed to be released from the charge of obscuring with our coats the back number-plate, and on several other occasions been in danger of being summoned for having no lights, when long past lighting-up time.

We were hurrying home one dark winter's night. It was on a Sunday, and we couldn't find a garage open that sold carbide, for in those early days we were foolish enough to start off without first attending to our generators, and we would not think of them until it was lighting-up time. We rode along in fear and trembling until, as we expected, we were stopped by a policeman. "Where are your lights?" he said, and we explained our predicament: to our surprise he was most sympathetic. "I should hurry home, if I was you," he advised, "before you meet a *policeman*!"

We had other similar adventures before we learnt to always keep our lamps and our generators full of carbide, while nowadays we are always very careful to see that our number-plate is not obscured, when we take a passenger on the pillion.

Another offence against the law is to leave a vehicle unattended, and if Eve wishes to leave her machine in the kerb for more than a few minutes, within sight of a policeman, it is a wise move for her to ask his permission. He usually is very nice about it, for he likes her to recognize his authority, and he will not only grant the desired permission, but he will also keep an eye on it while she is away. It is an offence to have the licence fixed on the machine anywhere where it is not visible from the left-hand side, and the law also demands that a motor-cycle shall have two brakes. She can have them both on the back wheel, but they must both work independently.

It is as well to remember that the law does not recognize ignorance, and that "I didn't know!" is not regarded by a magistrate as a good defence. It is the motorist's duty to know, just as it is the law's duty to prosecute offenders.

Before starting out, always make sure that you have in a handy pocket your driving licence, so that it will not be necessary partially to undress, if a policeman should ask to see it. If you have been careless enough to forget it, then you are quite safe if you can produce it within twenty-four hours; but this is only so by reason of police graciousness. The law demands that you should carry the licence.

CHAPTER XX

CLUBS AND THE SOCIAL SIDE

MANY girls who gaze with envious eyes at feminine possessors of motor-cycles would not hesitate to take the decisive step of purchasing one but for the fact that they dread the possibility of loneliness.

In the case of the girl who has no brothers and no near relatives or friends who are keen on the sport, this would appear a serious stumbling block, especially if none of her women friends are interested. A few years ago anyone who was so handicapped would have given up the alluring idea of owning a motor-cycle with a regretful sigh.

It would have seemed too impracticable. The idea of trying to teach herself to drive and becoming conversant with the technical side all by herself—would have been awe-inspiring. And then at the end of it all, having accomplished all these details, the prospect of long lonely rides, with no one to talk to or share meals with by the wayside, would not have the same thrill as planning excursions with interested companions.

All these disadvantages are removed by the advent of motor-cycle clubs. These are to be found in practically every district of the kingdom now, and they are a tremendous boon to all motor-cyclists. They serve to make the road-using fraternity into one huge family, while they foster the sympathy and friendliness which every rider feels towards all other members of the movement.

The motor-cycle club fills the great need of the social side; the committee arrange picnic runs and excursions for most of the week-ends during the season, and in the winter there are dances and whist drives, also, of course, the Annual Dinner, to which every member looks forward with keen delight.

The subscription to most of these clubs is extremely small, varying in amount from 7s. 6d. to a guinea, so that it is possible to belong to more than one, and so have the choice of alternative excursions, as well as twice the number of dances and such-like in the winter. There is usually a club in one's own town, and another within 10 miles or so, while in London there are any amount to choose from.

We are members of about eight in various parts of the country, so we find it very cheery when far from home to drop in at one of our club's headquarters and receive a hearty welcome from

72 MOTOR-CYCLING FOR WOMEN

the officials. The difficulty is in getting away again, for they are so hospitable, particularly in the North, that they simply cannot do enough to show how glad they are to see us.

Then, too, clubs are always extending invitations to each other to join in trials, gymkhanas, picnic runs, etc. This widens the

FIG. 23. WE STOPPED FOR COFFEE AT ABOUT 3 A.M.

field of one's acquaintances considerably, and the bogey of loneliness need never crop up. Ladies are warmly invited to join every club in the country except one (the Motor-cycle Club), and there is every hope that some day even they will discard their old-fashioned prejudices and admit women into their charmed circle.

Perhaps, because they are barred from this old-established club, it was felt that now there are so many women on the road

CLUBS AND THE SOCIAL SIDE

they deserved clubs of their own, to prove how well and ably they could run them.

Whether this is the case or not, there are now two flourishing clubs composed of and run by women, one in London, and one in Yorkshire. The Yorkshire Ladies M.C.C. is very friendly towards the London Ladies M.C.C., and invites them to participate in its trials, and the London Ladies M.C.C. responds in like manner.

For Photos

FIG. 24. THERE IS NO NEED FOR THE GIRL RIDER TO BE LONELY

We are members of the London Ladies, and our experience of it proves that it is a great step in the right direction. The membership is fairly small as yet, but it is steadily growing, and the comradeship and friendliness extended to all new members shows the spirit in which this club is run.

Any girl new to motor-cycling should take advantage of its facilities; indeed, it would be quite a good thing to join while contemplating buying the first motor-cycle: quite a lot of useful tips could be gleaned as to the type of machine most suitable. The new member could discover which make of machine and horse-power was chosen by other girls of her physique, and she would find plenty of fellow members willing and eager to help her with any information. She would find no difficulty in securing assistance in her first driving lessons, and help concerning the running of the engine, upkeep, and the hundred and one things necessary for her to know, would be hers for the asking.

By being a member of a club, it is simple to find a congenial companion for holidays or tours; everybody gets to know and like one another; they sort themselves out, and those whose pockets and temperaments fit naturally drift together, and make their plans accordingly.

All clubs have badges and discs which are supplied to their members for a small charge; these affixed to the mudguard or handlebars according to which type is supplied, signifies one's *bona fides* to any other members on the road. Our Ladies club makes a speciality of running picnics to which the participants bring their own food. This is a great scheme, since it makes the run so inexpensive that it is bound to suit every pocket. It is much more amusing when there is a big party, to picnic in a wood or a field with possibly a cottage handy for a hot-water supply, than to proceed in a dignified cortège to a swagger hotel. It makes it possible to the member who has little money to spend on her amusements, to enjoy every week-end, and not feel hopelessly out of it in attempting to live up to her richer sister's income. Some of these trips are bathing expeditions, and all members are notified to bring their costumes as well as their rations.

Then there are occasional week-ends at the sea, with accommodation arranged for beforehand by the officials. This is invariably good, and much more reasonable than a girl on a solitary trip hopes for. One of our clubs planned a delightful jaunt this year. They chose a night when the moon was full and, after supper at a popular restaurant, set off at 1 a.m. for Margate. There was a stop for coffee about three, supplied by a friendly garage, and we sauntered into Margate about 5 o'clock on a beautiful Sunday morning. We were very orderly, and taking care not to wake the inhabitants with undue noise, we made our way to the beach. A glorious early morning dip freshened us up, and by the time our 7 o'clock breakfast was ready we were ravenous. We spent the greater part of the day on the shore, and the braver spirits amongst us bathed again. Starting back about four and having tea *en route*, we were all home soon after eight, and everyone was unanimous in saying we never spent a more enjoyable day at such a little cost.

CHAPTER XXI

THE ART OF TRIALS RIDING

TRIALS riding is in a field of its own. It demands lots of practice, riding ability, strength, and courage, but the joys of conquest are very sweet. Constant riding is essential, and it is when experimenting and testing one's capabilities on difficult ground that the great boon of possessing brothers or other male impedimenta is felt.

When starting out to do a little practice on " colonial " sections, it takes a brave girl to tackle a steep and muddy track if she is all alone. She wonders if she will get stuck half-way and not be able to start up again ; and then there is the getting down these fearsome heights. No small matter to the girl whose experience is limited to main roads, or at worst, to ordinary country lanes.

But with a man to jeer or encourage, and demonstrate how such hills should be negotiated half the initial stage-fright is banished.

Two or three girls setting out together (if no man is available) can accomplish much. They can take it in turns to try to climb a difficult hill, and if the climber comes to a standstill, the others can hold the machine while she starts the engine and makes another attempt.

In this way they can all keep on practising, and learn how to pick their way, become skilful at avoiding boulders, take hairpins wide whenever possible, and keep their feet on the footrests in difficult circumstances.

It will be very good practice on attaining the summit to learn to come down and keep the machine under control. This requires quite an amount of skill if the hill is steep and muddy. Low gear and a delicate use of the front brake are the chief factors for success. A certain amount of " wind up " in the beginner causes a tendency to apply the brakes too abruptly, with a resultant skid and probably a fall.

These little tosses never hurt anybody, luckily, since the mud which causes them is nice and soft to fall on, and as the bicycle invariably slides sideways one subsides gently if not gracefully.

There are various methods of trying to climb a freak hill. One is to rush it, open the throttle, sit tight, and hope for the best. If the hill is short, very steep, and covered with deep mud, this is the only way to negotiate it, as taking it slowly one is apt to develop wheel-spin and come to a standstill through no fault of the engine.

The beginner, however, should stick to the slow and steady

climb for ordinary loose and rough gradients. It requires an almost super-human amount of skill to get round a hairpin at speed, whereas a neat, clean climb can usually be made by taking a hill with caution and judgment.

Always give an extra half-turn to the oiling system when approaching an " observed " hill. Very often it is quite impossible to spare a hand to give the engine a necessary pumpful when one is fully occupied with guiding the machine and keeping it on its wheels.

Learning to ride to schedule is a matter of experience, and is most necessary in these days when the winning of a chief award is often decided by seconds. A reliable watch is essential. We always wear ours around our necks on a cord, so that they are easy to get at. Route-card holders slung around the shoulders are much more satisfactory than having them fixed on the handlebars. The vibration makes it impossible to read the small print, but hanging at one's side it is easy to pick up and glance at the route-card without having to stop. This is a great help when heavy rain has washed the dye away, or a mischievous wind has blown an arrow askew.

One of the most acute miseries of trials riding is losing the way, and it is a misfortune which happens to the most experienced at times. Trial routes lie over such uncharted ground at times that there is no hope of meeting anyone from whom to make any inquiries, and as any tiny path or even a field with an open gate might be the route, it can be very puzzling.

A curious feature is the loneliness. Except for finding little bunches of competitors waiting outside checks, one can travel for miles without sighting another rider. Then it is the little demon doubt creeps in, " Have I left the route somehow or other ?" and the blessed relief is wonderful when the next number to you comes hurtling by.

These are the occasions when an easily picked up route-card is a great help, and it is a good thing to cultivate the faculty of memorizing the rights and lefts in their correct order in the directions on the route-card.

A necessary point is to study carefully the rules of the Trial before starting out. Many a silver cup has been lost through a misapprehension of the exact regulations of some special test. It is half the battle to have them at one's finger-tips.

Water splashes are the downfall of many riders, beginners and others. There is only one way in which to attempt these hazards, and that is, slowly. Never try to rush a water splash ; such method can have only one result—abject and complete failure. The correct procedure is to engage bottom gear, descend the bank as gently as possible, and cross as slowly as is practicable without losing one's balance. It will help considerably to slip the clutch

FIG. 25. LADY RIDERS IN AN INTERNATIONAL "6-DAY TRIAL"

Fox Photos

in order to keep the revs. up, and, of course, it is necessary to accelerate to climb the bank on the opposite side.

Plasticine is very efficacious to protect the magneto from the water. Seal up the cover with this and do not omit to attend to the lead, as this is one of the most vulnerable spots ; the water has a tendency to run down it into the magneto.

Even heavy rain can get into it if not protected either by grease or plasticine.

We were once caught in a terrific thunderstorm when we were riding two up. Some people in a car took pity on us. They stopped and invited us to come into their huge limousine for shelter. The deluge was so frightful that we didn't wait to put the machine on its stand, but just leant it against the grass bank and rushed for shelter.

That was our undoing, for when the storm was over and we tried to start the engine we found never a sound of life.

A friendly " Pratt's " lorry came in sight and was hailed with joy. The driver hoisted the little machine on his tail-board, and gave us a lift to the nearest town, where the local expert dismantled the magneto.

It was simply flooded, and all the trouble was caused through neglecting to put the bicycle on its stand. It was leaning over rather much, and the driving rain was directing its full force on the unprotected magneto—a point we remembered on a similar occasion. Another thing to keep in mind is to go over all nuts and bolts before and after a trial, some of the " roads " one is called upon to traverse are enough to shake a bulldog from his grip.

The girl who decides to be a passenger instead of doing the actual driving has her own little part to play, and by being expert, can certainly claim to have a hand in the winning of awards. A famous rider we know, who invariably has his wife with him, always declares that she wins his silver cups and gold medals for him. Certainly, a passenger who can be relied on to keep absolutely accurate time is a boon and a blessing, and when she has mastered the arts of reading the route-card and calculating distances to a nicety she will be a complete joy. Also there are a few useful acrobatic feats such as leaning out on corners to keep the balance, or leaning the carrier side to assist on certain hills (if this happens to be allowed), and other little methods of help, but these she had better learn from her driver, as there are many utterly different ideas on the subject. We have found, when acting as passengers, that one of the most important duties appertaining to the rôle is that of having matches and cigarettes always handy. If on a particularly hectic section, they happen to get bumped down into the toe of the sidecar, and so are impossible to get at without stopping in a nonstop section, it seems to be regarded as a national disaster.

Fig. 26. A Typical Section of "Trials" Country

Fox Photos

When Eve is the driver in these events, whether with passenger machine or solo, she should remember the danger of wet feet. In some routes water splashes are not mentioned or else very lightly dealt with, consequently it comes as a distinct shock when she encounters a stream which, while not exactly hub-deep, is sufficient to drench her feet and ankles. Hutchinson waders are the only wear for these occasions—indeed, they are always useful on any trial, as they insure warm and happy feet no matter what the weather conditions.

A liberal use of embrocation on aching muscles before going to bed is a good tip. It takes all the stiffness away, and one feels fit for another two hundred gruelling miles the following day.

All clubs run trials of various degrees during the season, some to suit novices, others of a semi-sporting nature to suit the more advanced spirits. The Surbiton Club is among the well-known clubs in London, and is famous for its fairly run and sporting trials. Foremost in these is the far-famed " Grand Cup Trial," and though one would need to be fairly expert to win an award in this event, there is nothing unfair to machine or rider in its hazards , and one has the supreme satisfaction of succeeding in a first-class trial.

Still, it would be better for the novice to try her prentice hand at simple touring trials, and having achieved a measure of success, she can graduate to more difficult sections.

Night trials are most thrilling, and delightful if there is a moon and the night is warm.

In all-night riding the passenger has it in her power to make things very comfortable for her driver and herself. Comforting beverages in Thermos flasks can be arranged, and it is a very good thing to carry some whisky and milk in a flask. Even in summer it can be fearfully cold just before dawn, and this mixture, besides being exceedingly warming, seems to dispel the deadly sleepiness that often overtakes one at this hour. If she has her escort's personal comfort at heart, she will carry a spare pair of gloves for him, a most cheerful surprise if his own get sodden in unexpected rain.

She must remember to dress warmly for all-night riding—even in August the warmest evening can change beyond belief in the long night hours.

Trials riding, whether as driver or passenger, is full of thrills and excitements, and makes a delightful change from ordinary humdrum life. It is well worth while to ride all through the night in order to see the first pale streaks of dawn and the beauty of the sunrise, not to mention the glorious appetite for early breakfast that one achieves on these never-to-be-forgotten runs.

CHAPTER XXII

CONCLUSION

ON glancing through these pages the fact is brought home in full force of the usefulness and general utility of the modern motorcycle. We number amongst our motor-cycling friends women of all classes and stations, from girls who have plenty of money and leisure, who use their mounts as runabouts when they do not want the bother of driving and parking the car, to the hardworking business girl who uses it as a means to health and adventure. We know one who is a cashier in a bank, and she spends all her holidays awheel, getting the maximum amount of fresh air and pleasure for the minimum of cost. Another friend of ours who lives in the North is employed as a District Nurse, and she uses her motor-cycle when making her professional rounds, riding in all weathers over some of the roughest and wildest roads in Derbyshire ; roads that are too narrow and neglected for cars, and on which one seldom meets even a farm cart. We advise any business girl who lives a few miles out of town to invest in a motor-cycle, for she will find it both money-saving and health-giving. She will find it such a welcome change to be dependent no longer on stuffy trains and buses, but to enjoy instead a healthy, invigorating rush through the air ; provided she is well protected from the dust and rain, and her bike is fitted with legshields and a windscreen, she can doff her overalls and walk into the office looking as though she had just stepped out of a limousine.

Parking a motor-cycle is sometimes a problem, but there is usually a courtyard or passage where the business girl can safely leave her steed, so long as the wheel is padlocked, and if she has to leave it in the open, a waterproof sheet can be had for a few shillings. There are so many uses to which one can put a motor-cycle that it would be possible to lengthen this book considerably, but we will end here, and leave our readers to find out for themselves all the pleasures that await them, when they finally decide to take the plunge, and invest in a motor-cycle.

Milady's Machine

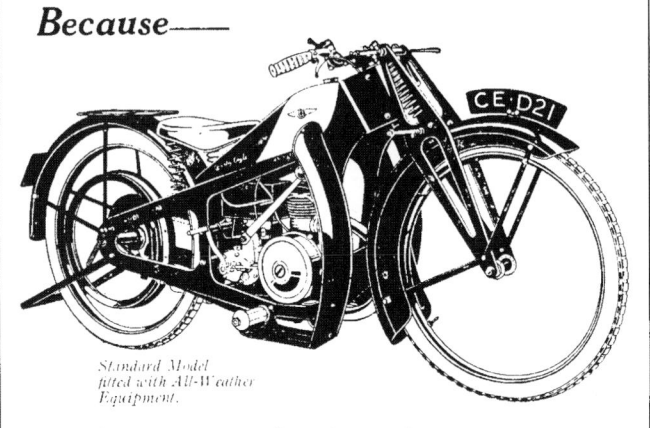

Because——

Standard Model fitted with All-Weather Equipment.

It's so easy to handle and control, so utterly reliable, light in weight, docile in traffic and flexible.

The Villiers Engine and simple patented channel steel construction render this machine without equal for reliability, accessibility and cleanliness.

Ample protection to machine and rider is afforded by All-Weather Equipment as shown, fitted to any model for the extra sum of £1.

Standard (147 c.c.) . **25 Guineas**
Tourist (172 c.c.) . . **£27 15s.**
De Luxe Super Sports (172 c.c.) **£35 15s.**

Coventry-Eagle

CYCLE AND MOTOR CO. LTD.

COVENTRY

Lady Riders defy the elements, with

HUTCHINSON
PONCHOS AND WADERS

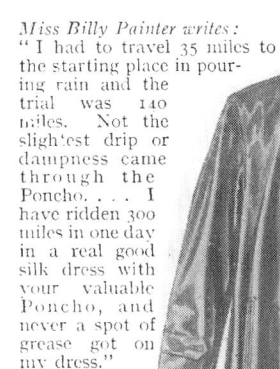

Miss Billy Painter writes:
"I had to travel 35 miles to the starting place in pouring rain and the trial was 140 miles. Not the slightest drip or dampness came through the Poncho.... I have ridden 300 miles in one day in a real good silk dress with your valuable Poncho, and never a spot of grease got on my dress."

MODEL B
Made from best Black Waterproof Materials. Shaped well at shoulder. Wind cuffs inside sleeve. 45″ and 54″ long.
36s. 6d.

WATERPROOF GAITERS
in Tan Leatherette. Lengths 15″, 16″, 17″.

HUTCHINSON WADERS
Absolutely wind, rain and dustproof. Worn over ordinary footwear. Full Hip length. Leather Soles.
Per pair
29s. 6d.

Write for Complete List to
HUTCHINSON HOUSE
119/125 Whitfield Street, London, W.1

Patented at Home and Abroad

a Cushion of SPRINGS!

—a source of endless comfort

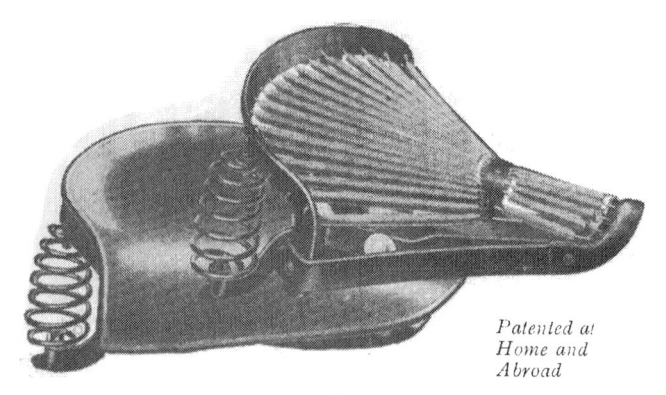

RIDE a "TERRY" de Luxe, and make sure of the wonderful luxury of healthy riding— free from nerve strain or saddle soreness.

Note how the spring seat is underslung on a slope-away back. It is impossible to bump hard anywhere.

> "We have enjoyed 'Terry' saddle comfort for two years on our B.S.A. machines, and we think them the most comfortable saddles."—Nancy and Betty Debenham

14" × 14", 45s.   13" × 13", 39s.   Pillion seats, 47s. 6d., 41s. 6d.
Specify for the new machine, or for the one you have.   List free

TERRY'S

Herbert Terry & Sons, Ltd., Manufacturers
Redditch, Eng.   Est. 1855

TRADE MARK

Utility · Pleasure · Economy

The Ideal Motor-Cycle for Women is the $1\frac{1}{2}$ H.P.

Francis-Barnett

The MODEL No. 4, complete with Electric Lighting, Leg Shields, Carrier, $2\frac{1}{8}''$ Dunlop Tyres, and Terry Spring Seat, is dependable, efficient, economical, safe, and comfortable.

This machine will do 35 m.p.h. and 140 m.p.g. The low riding position affords perfect control and imparts at once a feeling of security. Any cyclist can master the machine with half-an-hour's practice.

MODEL No. 4

£29

We also build $1\frac{3}{4}$ H.P. machines—Sports and Super-Sports Models, at £32 and £36 respectively. These models are capable of higher speeds and have won a great reputation in the principal reliability trials.

Catalogue post free on request

FRANCIS & BARNETT, LTD., COVENTRY

The most successful plug for motor-cycles

THE
LODGE
SPORTS PLUG

(Model H1)

Lodge Sports (H1)
6/-
Sold everywhere

Motor Bicycle Building 1906
by Hasluck
160 pages 137 Diagrams

The book is full of useful and detailed advice on building a pioneer motorcycle from scratch.

'The first thing to do will be to make a full-size working drawing on the wall or floor of the workshop where it will not readily be rubbed out.'

Introduction Buying a motorcycle in the early 20th century was a comparatively expensive business and reserved for the wealthier in society. For example, a Harley Davidson cost $200 in 1903 when the average wage was just 22¢ per hour: this was equivalent to two years wages for many people. Realising that many people had the skills to build their own motorcycle but not the cash to buy one, Paul Hasluck wrote "Motor Bicycle Building" in 1906.

Available now at £19.99
Free UK postage
classicmotorcyclemanuals.com
5 Quarry Lane
South Shields
NE34 7NJ
0191 435 4122
e mail and paypal
 steve@classicmotorcyclemanuals.com
Cheques payable to S Brown

Feedback

'Thanks a good read'
'Great book'
'Very prompt postage, good book'
'Very please with item, very fast dispatch, all good

The Motor Cyclist's Handbook 1911 by Phoenix

Written by a young motorcycle engineer for the layman in 1911 this profusely illustrated book is an absolute joy for anyone interested in the development, design and the maintenance of veteran motorcycles. A great piece of Social history reproduced as a good quality hardback book for your enjoyment. Full of references to, or adverts for Chater Lea, Douglas, Montgomery, Triumph, Hobart, IVY, NSU, Peugeot, Rex, Premier, JAP, Scott, Arno, Norton, NSU, Motor Reve, BAT, FN, Wanderer, Zenith Motorcycles, AMAC, B & B, JAP and Longuemare Carbs, Bosch Magnetos, Jones Speedo, Dunhill Acetylene Lights, Armstrong Triplex Three speed Gear.

Available now at £19.99

Free UK postage
classicmotorcyclemanuals.com
5 Quarry Lane
South Shields
NE34 7NJ
0191 435 4122
e mail and paypal
steve@classicmotorcyclemanuals.com
Cheques payable to S Brown

Feedback

'Everyone at the shop impressed by the book (Veralls)'.
Ian Hatton
Hi Steve, The book has arrived safely today, highly delighted, thanks.
Jim L. Dunblane
'I just received my copy and enjoyed it so much, that the one I have just purchased I would like to send to my friend............'
Zac, Bermuda

THE MOTOR-CYCLIST'S LIBRARY

MOTOR-CYCLING *for* WOMEN

BETTY & NANCY DEBENHAM

Ladies!

you can forget the engine — just leave it to

Wakefield Castrol

undoubtedly the best method of keeping your engine in tune with the minimum of attention.

Ask any experienced motor-cyclist what oil he uses and the answer will invariably be "CASTROL" because it is the oil that the experts have made famous.

Enjoy your motor=cycling to the full by following the advice of 239 Leading Motor Manufacturers who recommend—

WAKEFIELD Castrol Regd. MOTOR OIL

—the Product of an All=British Firm.

C. C. WAKEFIELD & Co., Ltd., Wakefield House, Cheapside, London, E.C.2